BHAROSHA MA

22 Weeks With Divinity

Gwyn McGee

Beyond Maya Press

Copyright © 2009 Gwyn F. McGee

All rights reserved

No part of this book may be reproduced, or stored in a retrieval system, or transmitted in any form or by any means, electronic, mechanical, photocopying, recording, or otherwise, without express written permission of the publisher.

ISBN-13: 978-0-615-33507-0

Cover design by: Steven Patterson
Printed in the United States of America

In 2009, I met Bharosha Ma in Puttaparthi, India. There, Sri Sathya Sai Baba blessed this manuscript with vibhuti. This Book Is Dedicated To The Purna Avatar.

Acknowledgements

I want to acknowledge and thank the following people for their generous hearts:
Steven L. Patterson for his artistic vision which shines brightly in the cover for this book. Beverly Poitier-Henderson, for her friendship and editorial insight. Rhonda Hinds, for her kindness and scrutiny. Jacquelyn Dropek for loving photography and sharing that love with me and this project. Hazel Smith, for years of carrying the baton in my parade when I could not see the parade. And my husband, Larry, for his love, and for paving a smooth road for my spiritual journey in this lifetime.

PROLOGUE

1988 was a pivotal year in my life. I was a practicing Buddhist in Memphis, Tennessee, and had developed a budding friendship with a woman named Pamela Drinnon. At the time I had major financial troubles, that was the norm, and I did not have the money to pay a cut off notice issued by the utility company. The day before the deadline I knocked on doors in a wealthy neighborhood hoping to do some housework for the day, but all of the residences I approached employed maids. So my sole solution for the problem was to stay up and chant, Nam-myoho-rege-kyo all night if I could. To my utter surprise, the next morning Pamela contacted me and told me her sister, LaVern McKarem, who still rises and meditates at 4:00 a.m. every morning, told her my voice...my cry out to the Universe was so strong that she felt compelled to send me $100.00. Mind you, I had never met LaVern, and Pamela may have mentioned her sister to me, but I don't recall it if she did. I do know LaVern was never the focus of our new, developing acquaintance and conversations. I was totally unaware of LaVern's spiritual practices and that she knew I existed.

After she sent me the money, I didn't physically meet LaVern until months later; when my life took a dramatic turn. That turn occurred after a man broke into my home at 4:30 in the morning; I woke up to a flashlight in my face, and a sweaty, obviously unstable stranger demanding money as he held a hammer over my head.

I came through that experience unharmed physically, which is amazing, but emotionally I was a wreck, and I became angry at God for allowing me to experience such trauma when I was trying to live a respectable life. With hindsight, I see the tremendous grace that permeated that event. For whatever reason, that night, before I went to bed, I put on a brand new, floor length gown, and I placed all my bill money under a platter on my dresser; two things I'd never done before.

The break-in occurred on September 18, 1988, and I raged at God for days after that, despite my Buddhist belief in an orderly universe that did not focus on God's compassion. But at that time I needed that compassion. I needed it so badly and I challenged God for it. I said if I was living a life strictly under the Law of Karma I didn't want it anymore. I wanted the Law of Grace and I demanded it be given to me right away. For several days, every day, something would just hit me in my heart and I would scream at the top of my lungs at God. As blasphemous as that might sound to some; I was angry, and that's how I felt.

And then, one month later to the day, October 18, 1988, I met my current husband, Larry, and my life took a tremendous turn for the better.

The traumatic break-in was a catalyst. That life quaking event forced me to realize I needed answers to questions that had not been answered to my satisfaction through the religious experiences I'd had thus far. And that's how I met LaVern. I attended a dream seminar that she facilitated at her sister, Pamela's home. As a result I've kept a dream journal more on than off ever since.

After the seminar Lavern and I kept in contact. My admiration for her grew, and I deeply appreciated the spiritual insights she shared during our conversations. It was a result of that relationship, and because LaVern is a reverend, that Larry and I decided that we wanted her to perform our wedding vows that following September, 1989.

During a wedding preparation meeting in LaVern's meditation room, I noticed a photograph of a man with a profusion of dark hair among a collection of other interesting items. I asked who that man was. She told me it was Sathya Sai Baba, and that she'd actually gone to India and had seen him in person.

Before I left that day LaVern gave me a small container of vibhuti, a kind of ash that Sai Baba was known for creating with a wave of his hand. It was his calling card; a reminder of the impermanence of physical reality, she said. You know dust-to-dust? I remember looking at it and thinking how it reminded me of the ash that accumulates from burning incense. But LaVern said this Sai Baba was a God-being in our midst, an ***avatar*** who demonstrated unusual powers over physical reality. I was somewhat surprised by the description, but LaVern had gained my respect and I took her at her word.

Amazingly, Sai Baba appeared in my dream that night. He stood on the right hand side of an empty, wooden chair pointing toward a dusky pink rose painted near the top. He wore a white robe, and the same rose was on a necklace in the dream. But after that the truth is, I put the container of vibhuti on my dresser and I didn't give it or Sai Baba another thought until my wedding day a few weeks later.

The entire week prior to our outdoor wedding,

local and national weathermen predicted bad weather, and every day there were thunderstorms and rain. It was misting the morning of our wedding, then by early afternoon it began to rain and the weather turned very cool. A cold front was moving in, and the temperature was expected to drop continually throughout the day until it reached the upper 30s that night, which is unseasonably cold for Memphis in September. But I didn't need the weathermen's forecast to know something unusual was going on. All I had to do was look outside. It was nearly dark in the middle of the day, and as my husband-to-be and his best man, George Cannon, attempted to set up chairs in gusting winds and blowing rain, I became extremely anxious when they reentered the house on a couple of occasions to warm up by drinking coffee. We had envisioned an outdoor wedding in front of the lake behind our contemporary townhouse; a townhouse which could not comfortably hold the number of guests we expected.

Desperate, I began to pray out loud. To be honest, I was concerned about what Larry and George might think about me, but not concerned enough to stop. In the midst of my prayers, I thought of what LaVern had told me about Sathya Sai Baba, so I began to call out to him. I said, "If you are who they say you are, then you can do something about this weather. You can blow away the clouds and the high winds with a single breath." Yes, as you can probably tell by now I can be dramatic, and I wanted results.

So I challenged this so-called Avatar with all my heart. I also proclaimed, if my bond with Larry was a positive manifestation of Spirit...God, then my prayers would be answered. I asked that the weather be beautiful for at least two hours while our wedding took place. The ceremony was scheduled for 5:30 p.m. and I began my loud outpouring around 3 o'clock.

By approximately 4 p.m. I, along with Larry and George, was amazed to see a line as straight as an arrow, separating the black stormy front overhead from crystal blue sky that was moving toward us. By the time the wedding ceremony began, our guests were seated comfortably in spaghetti straps and other warm weather clothes, under a cloudless sky with a beaming sun.

After the ceremony, I quickly prepared to go to our hotel near the airport; we were flying to Paris, France the next day for our honeymoon. As I gathered my final items I thought of Sathya Sai Baba and the weather. Excited, I placed the container of vibhuti that LaVern had given to me in my purse, and secretly determined to meet someone in Paris who knew the Avatar. I was not disappointed.

Larry and I were in the Metro Center of the Paris subway station. On a couple of occasions we had used the subway to get around, but this time we were more than a little confused about which train to take. We were facing the wall looking at the subway map when I heard someone behind us ask, in French (I took French in my early years), "Can I help you?" It was the first time a stranger in Paris had initiated a conversation since we arrived, and he spoke to our backs.

When we turned around, a tall, very dark skinned man with naturally straight, black hair stood before us. I told Larry what he had said, and at first Larry was a little hesitant.

“Do you speak any English?” I asked because my French language skills had dwindled immensely.

“Yes,” he replied. “Where are you going?”

We told him our destination and he said, “Okay. Come with me."

We followed the man to an escalator. As we rode down to our subway train platform deep within the structure, I asked him where he was from. He was obviously not a native Frenchmen and his accent was quite different.

“I am from India,” he replied.

Immediately, I thought of Sathya Sai Baba. “What part of India?”

“The south of India,” he said.

At the time I knew Sai Baba was born, and actually still resides in the southern Indian city of Puttaparthi. “Do you know Sai Baba?” I asked.

His eyes widened. "Do you know Sai Baba? He gave me this ring.” He showed me his hand.

Astonished, I gawked at a remarkable ring featuring a king-like image of an Indian man. Overflowing with excitement as my bewildered husband watched, I blurted how I had secretly determined to meet someone in Paris who knew the Avatar.

“I have seen him manifest vibhuti,” he told me. “Many people in India believe in Sai Baba.”

I was astonished by the ‘coincidence’ of the encounter, but on top of that the man was unusually kind. He rode with us on the subway train until we got off, and offered an enthusiastic good-bye, waving from each window as the vehicle pulled away until we could no longer see him.

That was my introduction to Sai Baba, and

as amazing as they are to me as I write them here, at the time I still had no inclination to find out more about the Avatar. Thirteen years would pass before my interest would be rekindled.

CHAPTER 1

Salt Lake City is a beautiful town; a valley surrounded by the potent Wasatch Mountains. During my first spring there I began to call Salt Lake "the city of roses". Roses of numerous colors and sizes bloomed everywhere in the spring and sustained their aromatic process into the summer months. They flourished in the well groomed yards of public buildings and cherished homes as well as in overgrown lots dominated by dilapidated structures. It didn't seem to matter to a becoming rose where it bloomed in Salt Lake. I was very aware of their tremendous presence because I believe flowers are physical symbols of grace, and roses are the epitome of that grace.

I recall hearing on more than one occasion how some folks in the Salt Lake spiritual community viewed the Salt Lake valley as an energetic bowl where people are given, might I even say graced with an opportunity to work on the deepest issues in their lives. That had certainly proven to be our experience, my husband Larry and me, during the short fifteen months that we had lived in Utah.

The events of this memoir commence in a rose filled Salt Lake summer in 2002. I was walking, enjoying the second leg of a trip to a spa called Parvati's in Trolley Square Mall where I was scheduled for a pedicure. I had taken a bus from our downtown apartment, but because of the established bus route I had to walk a few blocks.

Parvati's closed approximately a year later, but at the time it was a beautiful establishment. I discovered it during a previous trip to the mall when I asked a woman with a fetching mendhi...henna where she acquired the design. It turned out she was the mendhi artist and she worked part-time in the mall at Parvati's.

The spa was closed that day, but I decided to make an appointment after I looked through the shop window. It was tastefully decorated in a beautiful Indian décor. For whatever reason I can't recall a time when I didn't have a love for exotic things, and by looking through that window I could see that much time, thought and pride had been invested in the spa. So I made my first appointment at Parvati's, I believe it was in May of 2002. You see, I didn't start to keep a daily journal of the events that were unfolding until two months later in July. That's how I know it was on July 18th that what I'm about to write took place.

I had gotten off the bus and was walking down the street on my way to Parvati's when I heard a male voice speak to me. I heard the voice as clearly as you might hear a friend or your husband or your brother speaking if they were sitting or standing next to you. The voice said to me, "You are going to write a book. It will not be like the others. And it will be called 'The Altar'." It was not loud, but it was very clear.

Now. I need to establish something. I am not prone to hearing voices. I have no history of psychiatric imbalances, and those who consider themselves to be clairaudient (people able to hear voices or sounds that are not normally heard by the human ear) would not include me in their ranks by any stretch. Yet I stand on the fact that I heard what I heard and I can not deny it.

So I've just established one thing. I am not clairaudient. Now let me give a tiny glimpse of who I am. I am a person with a very open mind. I consider myself both a religious and spiritual person. My history includes being raised as an Episcopalian, experiencing life as a Muslim and life as a Buddhist. I've also attended spiritual ceremonies with Native American and Costa Rican friends. I guess you could say instead of going to a university and studying religions, I determined to spend at least 15 years of my life practicing and participating in a variety of them. At this point I am simply a person who believes unequivocally in a Supreme Being, and I honor and respect those whose lives reflect the religious or spiritual tenets that they believe.

So not being a clairaudient, I was totally surprised to hear a voice speaking to me. After the initial shock I also noted that it addressed me as "you". When I think about how and when this happened I'm certain anyone in a car that might have passed by at that moment, although I don't recall any, would have seen me searching for the source, although I knew there was no one near me.

I heard the voice as I approached the corner of 500 South and 700 East, a corner where Smith's grocery used to be. Although I knew I had heard the voice, it was so out-of-the-ordinary that what must have been seconds later I attempted to twist what I had heard. I remember thinking perhaps I had thought the words. But I knew that wasn't true because as I walked that morning I was not thinking about writing. I was enjoying the beautiful weather... the walk...the flowers, particularly the roses that were nearby. On top of that I could not ignore that the voice said "you" and not I, and how it was a male voice. The other fact is the voice said "You will write a book and it will not be like the others". At the time I was a fiction author writing under the pen name of Eboni Snoe with 12 novels to my credit.

Now, believe it or not when that happened to me, call it coping skills or whatever you want, I naturally pushed the event to the back of my mind. I guess I didn't know what else to do with it. When I think about the entire chapter of my life that I'm about to share with you now, I think it's amazing how we deal with things for which we have no logical fit. I knew I heard the voice. I tried to find a logical source. When I couldn't find one I attempted to brush what happened aside.

By the time I arrived at the spa maybe ten minutes later and was greeted by Janet Fredrick, Parvati's owner, I had placed the event on a mental back burner. From the very beginning Jan and I established an instant rapport when I recognized a photograph of Sathya Sai Baba that she had carefully placed on a shelf. We met thirteen years after I was introduced to the avatar.

That particular morning, after I heard the male voice, I immediately noticed Jan was a bit more excited than the calm, serene woman I had encountered during my previous visits. I was comfortably seated in a chair above a built-in basin that she had begun to fill with warm water before I began to understand why. Jan had sat down for her usual morning meditation, and surprisingly enough, received a message about me.

"I was told you are going to write a book and it would be about Bharosha."

I was stunned. I sat with the water running over my feet and tried to wrap my mind around what was transpiring. I had heard a male voice, perhaps twenty minutes earlier speak of a book, and now Jan had received a similar message that morning in meditation. Let me be clear. I had not told Jan about the voice I had heard, so for me all of this was very difficult to swallow.

"Bharosha," I repeated stupidly. "What's a Bharosha?"

Grinning, Jan left the room and returned with the book, Wake Up Laughing. She opened it to a colorful section of photographs, and pointed to a picture of an altar.

"This is an altar in Bharosha's home in Kathmandu," she said.

CHAPTER 2

Yes. Jan actually opened that book and pointed to a photograph of what I would call an altar.

"Bharosha is a woman who lives in Nepal," Jan began to explain.

I believe it was at that point that I told Jan about the voice I heard on my way to her spa. Remember, the voice said the book I'd write would be called 'The Altar', and here she was pointing to a photograph of what I interpreted to be an altar. Bharosha's altar!

We were very excited and amazed that we both received an unusual form of communication about the same subject: me and a book. Now I've come to see the term, altar, as a particular culture's description of a space with spiritual or religious items. In other cultures the collection of religious or spiritual objects would simply be an aspect of their prayer room. In the Hindi language a prayer room is called a ***puja*** room, and it includes what I would call an altar. But the point is; I didn't say Jan searched for the photo. She opened the book, the photo was one of five, and she pointed at a picture of what I perceived to be an altar a mere twenty minutes or so after I heard the voice.

Needless to say, my mind raced as I studied the photograph. I noticed a raised area with several objects including a large Krishna statue and a smaller Shiva statue. To the right of the photo there was a sizeable chair with a red slip cover decorated with a golden Ohm. There was also a substantial painting or poster in the background that was almost covered with some kind of gray matter.

"What's that?" I pointed to the substance.

"It's vibhuti," she replied. "It continuously comes on that painting."

When I looked down at the caption below the photograph it read, "Krishna statue in Bharosha Adhikari's home, which manifested butter that fed hundreds of people."

"She's a healer," Jan continued. "She started doing the healings after she died and Sai Baba brought her back to life."

You read that correctly. Jan told me Sai Baba had resurrected a Nepalese woman named Bharosha Adhikari.

At that point I didn't know what to say. I mean, what do you say? So much was going on that involved the extraordinary, and because of my past experiences with Sai Baba, I did not discredit what Jan said. I didn't exactly believe every word of it, but I didn't dismiss it either.

Although the face was small, I pointed at an attractive woman in another photograph. "Is this Bharosha?" There were four people in the shot. She was looking back at the camera.

"Yes, that's her. Her daughter, Sujata, lives right here in Salt Lake," Jan informed me. "I go to their house for ***bhajans*** (devotional singing) on Friday nights. Normally, it's just me and Sujata, her husband, Sarit, and their two children, Tina and Sanjay." Her face brightened even further. "But guess what? Bharosha is coming to Salt

Lake in September!"

"She is?" It was another bit of startling news.

"Yes, she is. Would you like to interview her?"

It was that simple. I believe Jan asked did I want to interview Bharosha because we were in the midst of an uncanny merging of circumstances and, because she was a giving individual. Jan also knew I was an author with several books under my belt, and I'm sure I'd told her I had been a news reporter in Memphis, Tennessee for several years. Well, I leaped at the opportunity she offered.

"I absolutely would," I replied without hesitation because I didn't need to be hit over the head. I intended to follow the signs, the yellow brick road that was unfolding before me.

Over the next few days I borrowed a couple of videos from Jan about Sai Baba: Aura of Divinity and Man of Miracles. I wanted to know more about this avatar who I had known **of** for thirteen years but never felt an inclination to really know; an avatar who people believed had brought Bharosha Adhikari back to life after death.

I found the videos fascinating and deeply moving. I loved the thought that there was someone here on the planet today that could do the things people said Sai Baba was able to do. Yes, I can say I believed some of it, but my logical mind wasn't so easily appeased. In other words I had definite doubts.

Today I view those doubts as a kind of fear, a fear of being duped as many are everyday when it comes to religion and spirituality. I didn't want to hand over my cherished belief in a spiritual power greater than myself to something or someone that was a mere mockery. Honestly... there **was** something inside of me that rejoiced in the possibility of a Sai Baba existing amongst us, but that didn't make his existence easy to believe.

So I was thrilled when Jan informed me during a subsequent visit to Parvati's that interviews had been arranged with the Adhikaris: Bharosha and her husband, Ramesh, as well as the Rimals: Sujata and her husband, Sarit. I'd be given an opportunity to speak with, and ask questions of a woman who remembered being resurrected by Sai Baba. I'd be able to look at her husband, her daughter and son-in-law in the eye and ask about Bharosha, and hopefully validate for myself if Sai Baba was truly an avatar.

It was exciting, but the subject matter was a sensitive one and I had no intention of disrespecting anyone in the process. How often does one get the chance to interview a person that has been brought back to life, not by medical means but by spiritual power? These were grounds where I intended to tread lightly, be it the truth or not.

In hindsight, I was absolutely naïve about the complexity of it all. I knew what I was delving into was profound, but because of the synchronicities that led up to the opportunity, I convinced myself that I was ready. I know now, I was not.

But what did I do back then? I went out and bought a small journal, one that would be easy to carry and not too overbearing. Now as I gaze at the orange cloth journal with its beaded rose cover, and even after I bought it, I felt the notebook was unusually appropriate for the task. The color was almost identical to the orange robe Sai Baba was known to wear, and as for the rose, it reminded me of the roses that appeared in my first dream of the Avatar, the night after I was introduced to him.

I heard that voice, the disembodied male voice, on

July 18, 2002. On July 24th Jan invited me to the Rimal's home. I would be allowed to take photographs and view the evidence that remained in the house after Bharosha Ma's last visit, six years prior. As I told you, I was told, after Bharosha Ma was brought back to life, she had been given healing abilities. I was also informed she returned as a vehicle for Sai Baba's manifestations. That meant with Bharosha Ma's presence, the vibhuti that he was known to manifest was said to appear on religious statues and photographs. Cum cum, a powder that ranged from vermillion red to burgundy would also appear. In other words, Bharosha Ma was said to be a catalyst for unusual physical manifestations. Jan had been to the Rimal's home. She had seen evidence that those assertions were true and she was inviting me to witness them.

The invitation came on a Wednesday, and that Friday, July 26th, Jan picked me up and we drove to the Rimal's for their weekly bhajans. Although the Rimals live in the Salt Lake valley their residence is actually situated in West Jordan, Utah.

It was a small gathering, the Rimal family, me, Jan and a woman who was a former Hare Krishna. When we arrived I was given a gracious welcome before Sujata and Sarit passed out numbered cards that determined who would sing bhajans, and in what order. Everyone received a card except for me.

It was all quite pleasant. The singing, cymbals and Indian drums, the smell of incense, and the Hindu traditions which included the waving of a live flame. At the end I watched Sujata come around with a salt shaker nearly full of vibhuti. She sprinkled it into offered right palms that were carefully placed upon the left palm. Sarit consumed some of the vibhuti he received and placed the remainder on his forehead. Similar actions were taken by the others. I offered my palm and hesitantly tasted the vibhuti. It was mild and floral.

Bhajans lasted about 30 minutes. Afterwards I was given permission to take photographs. In the puja room, there were several photos and posters of Sai Baba along with posters, paintings, and statues of other Hindu gods. But there were also framed images of figures and symbols from a variety of religions, from Christianity to Zoroastrianism.

Once the ceremony was over, Sujata offered to make chai tea. Sarit gave me a book about Sai Baba called Living Divinity, and he talked about the Avatar. Intuitively, I felt it was not the right time to ask questions about Bharosha Ma, so I simply listened. But once the tea was served there was a shift in formalities, and I managed to ask the Rimals about the vibhuti I saw on some of the photographs of Sai Baba. There was also a red streaky substance that covered a large portion of a poster of Durga, a Hindu goddess.

Sujata told me in straight forward terms that the vibhuti appeared the last time Bharosha Ma, her mother, visited her home. The streaks of red were a materialization of cum cum and amrita, a nectar sweeter than honey. She spoke of other startling manifestations. The one that grabbed my attention was Sujata's account of an ohm made of vibhuti that manifested underneath wax paper that was on top of a rice dessert called kheer. Sujata said the dish was still in the pot, on the stove.

Our first talk over tea was short. I did not press the Rimals with questions about Bharosha Ma. Somehow after such kind hospitality it didn't feel right to do so.

During our chat I remember repeatedly gazing at a shoulder-up photograph of Sai Baba with an ohm made of vibhuti over his head. The photo was placed high on a wall above an open arch that looked down into their puja room from the kitchen. I couldn't help but think that I had held some vibhuti in my hand minutes earlier, and how easily I could have blown it away with a breath. The ohm vibhuti that clung to the photograph defied gravity.

Needless to say my mind was extremely busy during the drive home, but my heart was exhilarated. I believed the Rimals were sincere, and that they were definitely devoted to their religious practice, but any belief that I had about the manifestations around Bharosha Ma and Sai Baba was cloudy. The remnants of vibhuti and cum cum and amrita could've been placed on the photos at any time, by the Rimals, even Bharosha Ma for all I knew. I guess what I'm saying is, it was too much for my logical mind to accept. I'd thought, perhaps, after visiting their home and seeing the "evidence" that I would be convinced that what Jan and the Rimals believed was true. But the truth is, although I believed something special was happening, the doubts were no less. The reason I believed at all was because I had experienced some unusual events around Sai Baba.

Personal experience is a powerful thing. When you've had a personal experience, no one can take that away. It doesn't matter what someone else might say or think. You know what you experienced and it is your truth. It was the strength of the Sai Baba experiences, of which I included the disembodied voice, which led me to the Rimal's home in the first place. Those experiences were powerful enough that I determined I would continue to go to their bhajans on Friday nights. What I realized was, I had a fond place in my heart for Sai Baba, avatar or not, and who knows where a feeling like that is born.

When I arrived home I re-read some sections about Bharosha Ma in Wake-Up Laughing. Afterwards I couldn't go to sleep. What if all of the things I'd been told were true? Although I'd had experiences involving Sai Baba and read of his "manifestations", they didn't seem as tangible as what was said to have occurred at the Rimals. And to be in a house where one woman's presence was the catalyst for startling manifestations....

Here in the United States we don't believe that physical matter can simply appear out of thin air. I'm not saying other cultures such as the Indian and Nepalese cultures don't believe in science and logic, they absolutely do. Yet as far as written human history goes those cultures have been known to accept realities beyond physical principles. By far the majority of Americans, those of us in the West in general, would stake our very lives on some things not being possible. Therefore, instant matter...or should I say, instant vibhuti? Not possible.

But yet the mystic in me asked: what if there was some energy or power unknown to science that could make this happen? What if?

One thing for certain was, if what the Rimals said was true, I knew it would shake and re-shape my view of reality, and that was a little frightening. So I wondered if I could handle it. I really thought about it. I concluded I didn't know if I could, but there was no way that I wasn't going to find out.

A few days later Jan informed me that Bharosha would not be coming in September. Sai Baba had requested that Bharosha come to Puttaparthi, the city where Sai Baba was born, first. She and Ramesh would stay at the ashram for one month; afterwards they would leave India and travel to the United States; first to Salt Lake City, then to Little Rock, Arkansas and Atlanta, Georgia. After that the Adhikaris would return to Utah, their home base during their stay in the States.

CHAPTER 3

I attended bhajans every Friday. I looked forward to it. I sincerely enjoyed Sujata's singing and the rhythmic stride that Sarit's voice brought to each song. Sanjay, the Rimal's, 10-year-old son, was quite good on the drums, and his sincerity when he sang was moving. But then there was the Nepalese chai after bhajans. Sujata and most of the time Tina, their 12-year-old daughter, at her mother's request, prepared it without exception.

On August 9, 2002, for the first time, I drove to the Rimal's house alone. It was the family, me, a Sri Lankan woman, Nidra, who were there that night. During chai Nidra wanted to hear some stories about Sai Baba, and as the Rimals talked a strange thing occurred. A strong, distinct smell of jasmine surrounded me. There is no doubt in my mind about it. It was unmistakable. Surprised, I interrupted whatever was being said and asked if anyone else could smell it. Nidra, who sat closest to me, said she could smell a slight hint of it, but no one else experienced it. I was totally taken aback. It was most pleasant but uncanny.

Eventually the subject turned to Bharosha Ma. Sujata and Sarit told us that a small group of people from Colorado sought out Bharosha Ma while they were at the ashram in Puttaparthi. One of them, a woman, had several cancerous lumps in her throat, but after three days of healings by Bharosha Ma the lumps went away. It was at that point that I discovered, after Bharosha Ma performs major healings, for two to three days she becomes ill as her body transmutes the poison and disposes of it. This was the kind of intriguing information that trickled out as I joined the Rimal's on a weekly basis. But before Bharosha Ma arrived, there was one talk over chai that held a special significance for me.

I had become quite comfortable with my visits to the Rimal's house. I have a knack for remembering tunes and had caught on to some of the simpler Hindi bhajans. I was more at ease with the overall situation, and like the Rimal's and a few others who attended bhajans, was preparing and simply waiting for Bharosha Ma and Rameshji's arrival in the United States.

Jan had sewn several beautiful chair covers for a large chair that was for Sai Baba. This armchair sat in a special place at the front of the puja room, and it was explained to me that many devotees had a similar chair in their prayer rooms.

I couldn't imagine it then but while Bharosha Ma was in town, those chair covers would be only one of many things that adorned the Rimal's puja room as special festivities took place. For me, at that time, the seat represented a way of honoring Sai Baba, but as time passed I came to see it quite differently.

One evening Sarit, Sujata and I were sitting at their dining table; I was the only one who attended bhajans outside of the family that night and I asked about one of their paintings. I had recognized the subject matter several weeks earlier. It was a rendition, on cloth, of the ring I had been shown in the Paris subway station, by the man who knew Sai Baba. Automatically I assumed, like the chair, that many devotees of Sai Baba had a similar painting.

"I've got a question about the painting of the ring," I began. "Do most devotees have that painting, or a similar painting, in their puja room?

Sarit and Sujata looked at me as if they didn't understand the question. So I repeated it, pointing, but they still appeared puzzled. I didn't know how else to voice it. It seemed like a simple question to me.

Finally Sujata said, "No they don't. That's a painting of a ring that Baba materialized for my father. It is the real Krishna. There are only two rings like that in the world."

"What?" Now I was puzzled. Could I have seen the only other ring like her father's in Paris? I was stumped. "I saw that exact ring on a man in Paris. He showed it to me as we were going down an escalator in a subway station."

Then I told the Rimal's about my Parisian experience. Up to that point I hadn't shared much about myself. There were so many interesting things to observe and talk about besides me.

"All of this time I've been thinking practically every Sai Baba devotee had a painting like yours," I confessed, "or some version of that image."

Sarit let go of a laugh I had come to recognize. "That was Baba," he said, laughing again as Sujata nodded. Then he repeated it. "That was Swami that you saw in the subway station."

For a moment I just stared at him. Was he joking?

He chuckled. "Sometimes Baba will come in different forms. That was Baba who showed you that ring."

I had no reply for that. I had come to know Sarit

in a very casual way over the last few weeks, and I considered him to be an intelligent man. But what do you say to someone who you feel has offered one of the most outlandish answers that you've ever heard, without disrespecting them? Nothing. That's what you'd probably say, and that's what I said. When it came to that answer, the other accounts about Bharosha Ma and Sai Baba didn't matter. There was no place in my psyche for what Sarit had just told me.

Weeks passed and the waiting for the Adhikaris continued. There were several unusual spiritual occurrences during that time, but they are not significant enough to write about, except for one.

I spoke to one person almost on a daily basis about what was unfolding around the Rimals. She was Waheedah Ali, a friend of mine who lived in Atlanta, Georgia. We'd known each other for more than 25 years. She'd been privy to some interesting spiritual twists and turns in my life and was a safe, receptive, sounding board. But beyond that, we had shared a remarkable experience that involved Sai Baba around the time that I discovered the spa, Parvati. Now, let me make it clear, Waheedah was no Sai Baba devotee. Basically, what she knew about Sai Baba had come from me. But during an extremely stressed time in her life, Sai Baba appeared to her with an answer to a problem that she desperately needed to solve, while she was in a dream-like state.

On this particular day I had been out and about. Our over-the-phone conversation about the Rimals and Bharosha Ma had been cut short, so I promised Waheedah that I would call her back once I returned home. When I got to my apartment I went directly to my bedroom to use the telephone in there. Once I entered the room I was immediately engulfed by the smell of vibhuti! It was so strong that I went directly to my altar where I do my personal prayers behind a shoji screen, to see if I had spilled anything. I didn't know what would have spilled, but at that moment it was the only logical explanation. Everything on my altar was in its proper place.

Now, how did I recognize the smell as vibhuti? I was no expert on the subject at that time, nor am I at this point, but vibhuti has a specific scent. It is light, floral-like, fragrant... yet full of matter, and when I first entered my bedroom the words, "I smell vibhuti," came out of my mouth. It was an instant recognition. But although that recognition was solid, it made no sense to my logical mind. I recall standing in the middle of the floor contemplating the source of the smell as the scent hung for perhaps 30 seconds. Then it gradually dissipated. These were the kinds of things that I experienced before Bharosha Ma arrived in Salt Lake City, and what I shared with Waheedah when I returned her phone call.

CHAPTER 4

On November 18, 2002, I, along with approximately twenty others, attended bhajans. Bharosha Ma and Rameshji were there.

The first time I laid eyes on Bharosha Ma, I remember the house felt very still and quiet. There were just the three of us, Bharosha Ma, Sujata and me. Bhajans would not begin for another thirty minutes.

I entered the puja room and they were sitting on the floor directly across from me. Bharosha Ma had a subdued color Nepalese shawl wrapped around her, and a set of at least twenty, vibrant red bracelets on her arm. I could feel her studying me as I approached. It's funny, but even if there had been other people in the room, I would have known who she was.

I don't recall how Sujata introduced us, but I do recall how Bharosha Ma's face appeared to me. Her complexion looked soft and fair, and her dark hair was arranged behind her. She was beautiful, and although her features were gentle, at that moment her eyes were intense and steady. I sat down in front of them and I'm sure I said something like how pleased I was to meet her at last, and she responded with a slight smile and a nod. Afterwards Bharosha Ma said something to Sujata in Nepali, who in turn said to me, "Mommie says you are a devoted and good soul. She says good things are in store for you."

I was truly surprised by her remark...and grateful. I don't know how I expected my introduction to Bharosha Ma would unfold, but I was deeply moved to know this powerfully spiritual woman saw me in such a light, and was kind enough to say so.

"Thank you," I replied to Bharosha Ma.

“Mommie doesn’t speak any English,” Sujata said.

“Oh.” I looked at her mother.

Bharosha Ma shook her head ever so slightly, which obviously meant although she didn’t speak any English she definitely understood some of it.

“Look, Gwyn.” Sujata gestured toward the front of the puja room. “Vibhuti is coming everywhere.”

I turned my gaze toward the main altar. First I noticed several of the Hindu god and goddess statues had been placed in crystal plates, and there was a grayish white ash accumulating on and at the base of a few of them. I tried to recall what they had looked like before Bharosha Ma arrived, but Sujata called out to me again.

“Look at the Krishna, Gwyn.” She was standing near a foot and a half high, ornately painted, marble statue of Krishna. Piled on his horizontal arm as he held his flute, was the largest accumulation of vibhuti. There was also vibhuti at Krishna’s feet.

I saw the Krishna but I was most fascinated by an amazingly bright red powder accruing on a smaller statue beside it. “Is this cum cum?” I asked.

“Yes,” Sujata said.

Bharosha Ma continued to sit quietly. She never moved from the spot where we were introduced.

I looked at all the objects, thinking of how the vibhuti and cum cum was supposed to have gotten there.

But when I saw the substances with my own eyes, I found the materialization explanation more difficult to believe... although a vast part of me did believe. It was difficult because the materializations were no longer a concept. This was physical matter.

You have to understand, I could not see the vibhuti or cum cumi accumulating. It wasn't manifesting like water pouring from a faucet, but the way the piles were shaped, slightly pyramidal, looked as if they were growing.

By then other attendees arrived and they brought flowers and fruit as offerings. Sujata greeted them, took the offerings, and arranged them on the altar. Bharosha Ma came and sat near the front of the prayer room. Through gesture she offered me a seat beside her before she picked up some of the fruit as if she were blessing it. I watched as Bharosha Ma silently greeted several new people and accepted some more bananas. After she accepted the fruit, Bharosha Ma placed them with the other offerings below the statues and photographs.

Moments later Sujata pointed. "Whose bananas are these?"

"They are mine," someone replied.

"Ohms are coming on your bananas," Sujata said excited.

Bharosha Ma looked at me as if to say, *yes it is true*, before she leaned in a direction that enabled me to see. Light brown marks that resembled a number three and were about an inch and half in size could be seen on several bananas in one of the bunches.

"And there are more ohms coming on these over here." Sujata pointed.

I was shocked and my logical mind reared its rebellious head. Instantly I wondered if the people who'd brought the bananas were "in" on some kind of scheme to fool the rest of us. I'm ashamed to admit it now but I even thought, did Bharosha Ma or someone take a pin and scratch the ohms on the peelings before the gathering? But when I looked at the people who had brought the fruit they were obviously elated by the manifestation, and Bharosha Ma had moved on. She was searching through a small book that contained some handwritten Nepali. She didn't appear to be the least bit occupied by the quiet but ongoing jubilation. Once everyone settled in, including Rameshji, a distinguished looking grey-haired man who took a seat in the back, bhajans began.

Bharosha Ma was one of the singers. Her voice was as sweet and gentle as Sujata's was powerful and beseeching. I sang too, and Bharosha Ma beamed and smiled showing her approval. It is not easy to explain the thoughts and feelings that I experienced during that session, but something happened. I can't say what, but before I could hold them back a light flow of tears were on my face. I hadn't expected tears and I have to admit I was embarrassed by them. But when Bharosha Ma hugged me, I felt consoled and understood on a unique level, even though I did not understand my own actions.

Rameshji provided an explanation for my out-of-the-blue tears as many of the people formed a line to receive a healing from Bharosha Ma. He said something about when there is true devotion in the presence of divinity, eyes can not remain dry. I found his words very beautiful but, I was uncertain if they truly applied to me, although I hoped they did.

I watched Bharosha Ma place her hand on each individual after a short verbal exchange. On the spur of the moment, I decided to join the line. When it was my turn Sujata interpreted for me. I asked if I could simply receive a blessing. Bharosha Ma nodded, placed her hand on my head, and moved her lips with inaudible words.

After the healings, when the opportunity presented itself, Rameshji spoke with me at length. I soon realized he was attempting to know who I really was, what was in my heart, and what my intentions were when it came to writing a book about Bharosha. Finally, as it was getting late and we had barely scratched the surface, Rameshji asked me to return the next day an hour before bhajans, in order to talk some more. I complied, armed with a tape recorder in my purse.

CHAPTER 5

Tina opened the door when I arrived at the Rimal's at 6 p.m., and the smell of pleasant, but indecipherable spices wafted toward me. When I entered the kitchen I saw Bharosha Ma. She was standing at the stove cooking. She smiled as I spoke to her but turned back to her work when Rameshji invited me to join him in the living room.

We talked, and I presented my format for the book. I told him it would be called The Altar, and I'm certain I must have shared my experience with the voice that day, but as I write this memoir what I said is somewhat of a blur. Once again, I could tell Rameshji was attempting to discover my intentions, but at the same time share his insights about Bharosha Ma, their life, and some of the unusual things he had seen and experienced. Finally, I believe Rameshji concluded I was simply a novice in the world of Sai Baba, and that my intentions were good but I hadn't grasped the profundity of it all.

"You know Bharosha actually died," he said, "and that it was Sai Baba who brought her back to life."

"Yes, I've heard that," I replied. "I've also read some interesting things about her in Connie Shaw's, Wake Up Laughing. But there was so much it's rather difficult for my mind to absorb it all. But I do remember reading that you were in India with her when it happened."

"Yes." He nodded slowly. Bharosha and I were at

the ashram in Puttaparthi. It was in 1995. It happened on October 3rd.

Bhajans were being held and Bharosha was sitting in the women's section in the Abode of Peace. Baba came near to her and gave Bharosha what you might call a vision. She said there were lots of colors coming off of Swami. Very dazzling. Different beams of color. Baba looked like that." His eyes widened. "Shortly afterwards Bharosha fainted and was soon taken to the General Hospital, but I didn't know about it because I was sitting on the men's side.

I remember how Baba was walking around on our side, and I saw him stop and talk to Dr. Ayer. At the time all I could think was that I wish he would stop and talk to me. He glanced at me, but he kept going. Later I found out that Baba had sent Dr. Ayer to the hospital where Bharosha was so that he could attend to her. I heard he was weeping because Baba had sent him there, and Dr. Ayer was asking 'Where is daughter, Bharosha?'" Rameshji's brow wrinkled.

"When Bharosha was at the General Hospital they gave her some medicine, but after an hour her condition worsened. Dr. Kartkar was the General Hospital physician who was in charge. She told me Bharosha needed to be taken to the Super Specialty Hospital. Then I asked Dr. Kartkar, how can I just take her there." Rameshji paused. "Maybe they would give me some problems in admitting her. So she began to write a recommendation letter. But when Dr. Kartkar finished the letter and looked up, the man she was writing the letter to, was standing in front of her." Rameshji's face brightened as he spoke of the remarkable turn in events. "And she said something like, 'How is it that I am writing this letter to you and now you are here?' And the doctor gave her some reason. After that they talked, and he determined Bharosha had to have open heart surgery.

So we took Bharosha to the Super Specialty Hospital. Dr. K.P. Sharma was the surgeon there who was going to perform the surgery. He was about to begin when suddenly Bharosha had no vital signs. None." His eyebrows rose. "Soon after one of the doctors, he was very sad, said, 'She's no longer with us.'"

"Before he said that did they try to revive her?" I injected.

"Yes," Rameshji replied, "they tried, but finally they gave up." His dark eyes filled with sincerity. "I watched them lay Bharosha on the floor, and they chanted Om Sai Ram over her dead body."

"You must have been devastated," I said.

"I was in shock," he replied. "The grief was overwhelming but I had to carry on. There were things they wanted me to do. For instance the death certificate needed to be taken care of. And while Bharosha's body was still on the hospital floor the doctor filled it out and I signed it. Although he was sad for what had happened, he told me I had to remove the body because it couldn't be kept there."

"So, she was pronounced dead," I said. "There was an actual death certificate."

Rameshji nodded. "Yes, I signed it." His eyes brightened. 'But would you like to know what was going on while she was dead?"

My eyes narrowed. "I most certainly would."

"Bharosha told me as soon as she was out of her body dark entities came and began to attack her. They were biting her."

"Where did they come from?" I asked, alarmed.

"Perhaps it was another etheric realm or loka. But they were on her, and they began to beat her etheric body. She was terrified."

"I would be too," I said.

"Who would not be?" Rameshji's voice was as dense as a stone. "And now at the moment of death, Bharosha is alone defending herself, and she's doubting the worth of dedicating her life to Baba. But right then, she said snow began to fall, and in the direction that Bharosha was looking, there was a small red dot in the middle of the snowfall. Very quickly it grew larger, and all of a sudden Baba was there in his red silk robe. He told Bharosha to open her mouth, and out of his mouth he sent this flame. It was in the form of a yellow arch. After that Baba held her hand and quickly took her to a place of safety in another loka."

I was totally riveted by what Rameshji was saying, and I tried to picture it in my mind.

"There, in that realm, they went before a man who was going through the pages of a large registration book. Bharosha said there were maybe twelve other people there, and she said she watched Baba sign some kind of release paper. He also gave her etheric finger an injection." Rameshji sat back. "And do you know you could actually see where he injected her on her physical body when she came back.

"This is amazing," I said.

"Yes," Rameshji said. "But that is not all. Before Bharosha returned to her body in Puttaparthi, Baba told her he was removing her karma and extending her life. But Swami said there was a price. In order to be restored and her life extended Bharosha had to endure three things. When she returned she would have high blood pressure. She would have diabetes. And she would become a healer, a world-renowned healer. That would be the price of resurrection."

"She has those illnesses?" I asked.

"Of course," he replied. "Baba brought her back, but her struggle was not over. Bharosha could not speak for twenty six hours. She stayed in the hospital for sixteen days. But she had been through so much; a heart attack, leaving her body, dark entities attacking her."

CHAPTER 6

Bharosha Ma appeared in the opening between the kitchen and the living room. She motioned for us to come.

"Yes, we are on our way," Rameshji said before he summed up his talk. "And as you have witnessed tonight, Bharosha is fulfilling the third requirement. She is doing her healing work."

He rose from the couch. "Now it is time to eat."

I was acutely aware of the tape recorder in my purse that I had not used, but as before, I felt the time was not right for pulling out mechanical devices; so I followed Rameshji into the kitchen and at their bidding sat down to my first Nepalese dinner; a dinner prepared by Bharosha Ma. There were greens, steaming hot rice, a spicy side dish, and following Rameshji's lead I poured dahl, a soupy lentil, over my rice and ate the Nepalese way, with my fingers.

Bhajans proceeded as usual, but this time with my confidence bolstered I led an English bhajan, "Say The Name Of Sathya Sai". While we sang the unusual occurred again; ohms appeared on bananas and apples, and vibhuti manifested on photographs of relatives and individuals for whom attendees were seeking blessings.

As strange as it sounds, in the Rimal 's puja room these manifestations were just a part of it all. At least that's how it appeared to me. I noted there was no discussion over the validity of what was going on, nor were there any loud emotional acknowledgments. Why? Perhaps it was a matter of respect. It might also have been attributed to the fact that the majority of the attendee's ancestors, and many of them, had been born in the East. India. Sri Lanka. Nepal. Places where metaphysical and paranormal phenomena are known to occur, and are believed in and accepted from childhood.

At the end of bhajans the protocol from the previous night was repeated. Many people lined up and quietly received healings from Bharosha Ma. When they were over, Rameshji told a story that Sai Baba once told.

"Once there was a Black man who Whites would not allow in their church. He wanted to go in because he believed Jesus lived in there. Even when Jesus appeared to him outside the church, because he didn't look like the Black man expected, he still wanted to go inside. Finally, Jesus transformed into what the man expected." Then Rameshji added, "Sai Baba said the moral of the story is: God is not in a particular place or religion."

After bhajans a few of us stayed behind, and Rameshji expressed that they wanted me to write the book, but he didn't think I realized how important an undertaking it was. Years later, as I write this now, I can say that he was absolutely right.

As I left the house Bharosha Ma insisted that I take an apple with me. It had three ohms etched deeply into its skin. I remember excepting it gratefully like a child who'd been given something from a mother who sincerely wanted them to be happy. I was also grateful for the experiences I was having, and that my writing a book about Bharosha Ma had been accepted by all. As I walked out the door I promised Rameshji that I'd bring him one of my novels, so that he could read something I'd already written.

I got in my car but I didn't pull off right away. I sat in front of the Rimal's house with the interior light on studying my apple. The thought of what had happened to it amazed me. One of the ohms seemed to be burned, as if by laser, so deeply into the red outer cover that it sharply cut through the skin, and a hint of beige flesh could be seen.

When I arrived home I proudly showed the apple to my husband, Larry, before I cut it in half so we could share it. ***Prasad*** is what they called it; food that has been devoted to and blessed by God. Being at times a quiet, contemplative man, Larry accepted the apple and listened to what I had to say, but said nothing else.

CHAPTER 7

The following day I spoke to Jan on the telephone. In spite of the fact that her family was going through some challenging times that required much of her energy, she had a fascinating account to tell me.

Being the creative person that she is, Jan had sewn several ornate chair covers for Sai Baba's chair in the Rimal 's puja room. She had given them to Sujata at bhajans the day before and Sujata had stored them in a hall closet.

"About an hour or so ago," Jan informed me, "Ramesh asked Sujata if I had delivered the covers, and she told him, 'Yes'. So she went to the closet to get them and Sujata couldn't believe what she saw. Baba's hand prints were on every cover!"

"What do you mean hand prints?" I asked.

"His hand print," Jan repeated. "It looks like he has placed his hands in vibhuti, and pressed them against every chair cover." She chuckled vigorously. "Sujata said she was so overwhelmed that she fell to her knees in tears at the sight of them."

You can only imagine something that affected Sujata profoundly, someone who had experienced lots of phenomenon surrounding Sai Baba and her mother, totally baffled me. Hand prints appearing on cloth in closets??? I couldn't wait to see the things Jan had spoken of with my own eyes.

"And I've got something else to tell you."

"What?" I couldn't imagine what could top the hand prints.

"Sujata and Bharosha Mommie were talking, and Mommie told her that she loved you."

I felt an energy move in my heart, but I replied, "I'm sure she loves everyone who comes around her."

"That might be true too," Jan said. "But Mommie said she loves you. That you have touched her heart in a special way."

The truth is I knew that Bharosha Ma seemed to cater to me, that I felt a special energy between us, and now Jan had validated that.

Later I recall thinking, why are two people immediately drawn to one another? I couldn't help but believe with a spiritually evolved person like Bharosha Ma, that we must have developed a close karmic bond in the past. The past I am referring to is a previous lifetime... or even lifetimes. Years later it would be Rameshji who actually voiced his belief in just that. But at that time all I knew was, I liked the woman, Bharosha Ma, and I wished that we could speak one on one, and that there was no language barrier between us.

I arrived an hour early for bhajans that evening and Sujata was so excited she met me at the door.

"You are not going to believe what you are about to see," she said as I entered the house.

I had some fruit and a gift for the Rimal's in my hand; an ornate container I had purchased from a Jewish synagogue. Judaism was the only major religion that I did not see represented on their shrine.

"Come. Come." Sujata insisted. "You must see this."

I entered the puja room and Bharosha Ma was there. We spoke, and then I immediately looked at the altar. On a life-size poster of Sai Baba in an orange robe was a huge ohm symbol made of vibhuti that simply defied gravity! The ohm was perhaps fourteen inches in height.

And wouldn't you know it, I just measured it from a photo to guestimate the width for this paragraph...and at its widest point it is exactly the same measurement as the height.

At the Rimal's Sujata said, "Can you believe this, Gwyn? When I saw it I screamed and screamed." She mimicked her reaction.

I shook my head because it was difficult to believe. Then I looked at the poster of Shirdi Sai Baba beside Sathya Sai Baba. Shirdi Sai Baba according to Sathya Sai Baba was his previous incarnation, and on that poster were large Hindi letters written right across the center.

But that wasn't all. There was a profusion of vibhuti on the majority of the framed images of religious figures that surrounded the larger posters. Some of the smaller framed images had a sprinkling of vibhuti from when Bharosha Ma first arrived, but now it was as if the Big Bang had occurred in the form of vibhuti and increased the manifestations.

I tried to take it all in. But this vibhuti, this ash that was as fine as the finest flour was clinging to posters in a raised fashion as it formed the ohm and Hindi letters. There was no vibhuti outside of the perfectly formed characters. I knew, based upon the nature of the substance that was used to form these images, it would be humanly impossible to create.

"Oh my, God." I repeated softly. "Oh my, God,"

“And look, Gwyn.” Sujata motioned toward the footstool that sat in front of Sai Baba's chair.

There were footprints of vibhuti on top of the stool and on the slender decorative cloth walkway that led up to it. When I say footprints I mean it was the image of the bottom of a foot, that looked as if it had been placed into vibhuti then pressed against the cloth.

At that point Bharosha Ma took my arm and led me to a photo of Sai Baba's feet. She outlined some natural creases on the bottom of his foot, and then she motioned toward the vibhuti footprints. Bharosha Ma wanted me to compare the two. She wanted me to see that the footprints of vibhuti matched the bottom of Sai Baba's foot. I felt she was saying, this was proof that Sai Baba had actually been there. She wanted me to understand that the footprints of vibhuti were not hers or Sujata's or someone else in the Rimal's household. The vibhuti footprints were Sai Baba's. Afterwards she took the apples from me and placed them on the altar.

By then Sarit entered the room chuckling. He asked me what I thought about what had taken place. The truth is I have no idea what I told him. I do remember being at a lost for words after I gave him the gift.

As my thoughts rushed about chaotically, I sat against one of the walls in the puja room and watched as various people came in, noting their reaction's to the phenomenon. By now the crowd was numbering around thirty people every night. Still there were no loud outbursts, but the vibhuti manifestations did create a low, steady current of excitement as people took their seats.

I marveled at the restraint of the people in the room and before I knew it I was weeping. As before I don't know where the tears came from, but unlike the previous time, this time I wept on and off throughout the entire evening. It was as if someone had turned on a faucet inside of me and I could not turn it off.

When I recall what was going on inside of me, I was thinking about what was unfolding, and my heart told me it was real, even as my mind said **IF** this is real, how can **YOU** write about it? The question that surfaced was, and this was truly my thought, what makes you worthy of writing about it? If what was happening **was** real, I didn't know if I had the ability to write about the subject matter, and the capability to honor it. Yes, I'm an author. Yes, I had written many books. But this was one I didn't want to get wrong in the slightest way.

I gingerly expressed my feelings of inadequacy to Sarit and Sujata, and they attempted to encourage me with a story about a man who built an entire temple by himself. I listened, I heard what they said, but it didn't stop my tears.

By now the apples that I brought, that had been placed on the altar by Bharosha Ma had ohms on them, and some bananas offered by a long-time, elderly devotee had more ohms than I had seen on any of the fruit. Throughout the evening Bharosha Ma gave me what felt to be special attention, especially after I sang the bhajan. "Light In Me A Flame". She reached out and gently touched my throat, then touched her own throat before she touched her heart.

Bharosha Ma performed many healings that evening and when she was done she sat beside me and placed her hand on my knee. I felt so much for this woman whose very presence inspired faith, and through whom Sai Baba, a ***purna avatar***, a God-being of the highest power, seemed to effortlessly allow his manifestations to flow.

I had noticed times when her body seemed to tire from the healings, but she continued quietly with what felt like a silent resolve. Never did Bharosha Ma appear to be excited or moved in any way by the attention she was given as a result of what her presence brought. There was no pride in her eyes. She was silent duty and I loved her for that. That evening I couldn't help but tell her so.

"I love you," I said, my eyes swelling from crying.

"I love you," she said, her eyes full of sincerity. It was the first time I ever heard Bharosha Ma speak English.

By the time I arrived home with ohmed apples that Bharosha Ma insisted that I take, my eyes were very puffy. Larry greeted me when I came into our living room. He took one look at me and said, "You're sleepy".

"No," I replied, "I'm weepy."

I told him everything that had unfolded that evening, and when I was done he decided that he would attend bhajans with me the following night.

CHAPTER 8

As he said he would, my husband accompanied me to the Rimal's house the following night. I introduced him to everyone, and while Larry chatted with Sarit, Sujata led me to the altar. She picked up an apple that was sitting at the very front near the edge of the glass table.

"Gwyn look," she said, pointing at and reading what I assumed was four Hindi words. "Baba wrote, I love you, Sujata. See? I was so excited when I saw it. Oh my God, I cried and cried. I love you, Sujata." She read the words again.

I looked at the uniformed markings that formed a straight line around the curvature of the apple. They were approximately a half of an inch in height, and had been carved into the apple in same manner as the ohms.

Now this new turn in manifestations sent my logical mind to the place where it always seemed to go whenever something I had not conceived of occurred. It asked, "Did this really happen? Or was this an elaborate hoax?" Then my mind would go through what might be the motivation if it was a hoax. Money? But money couldn't have been it because I knew Bharosha Ma did not charge for the healings she administered, although there were people who offered gifts of various sorts from time to time. Monetary compensation or gifts were not requested. I even knew of instances when money had been turned down. So with this knowledge, again I asked myself, why would they stage such an elaborate hoax? For the attention, maybe? As I sit here now, years later writing this account, I can tell you without hesitation that a part of Bharosha Ma and Sujata would prefer a "more normal" existence. Attention was not their source of motivation.

There were at least fifty people attending bhajans that night. There was also a definite air of excitement or perhaps I should label it anticipation. Larry and I talked to several people, and I showed him the ohms that had appeared on some of the bananas.

One of the most impressive reactions to the phenomenon came from a young man who was a friend of Jan's. His name was Lee. He was also known as Sebastian. From what I could glean, Jan told him what was happening at the Rimal's home, invited him to come and he took her up on it. He also brought bananas as an offering. I'll never forget the look on that young man's face when ohms appeared on the bananas that he offered. He was so totally shocked that his face paled. You see, he was one of the very few who was not a Hindu. Like Jan, myself and Larry, he had no roots in Eastern culture, and therefore his novice reaction to the phenomenon effected me in a way that touched home.

After that more people came and Rameshji and Larry talked extensively. While they talked Bharosha Ma invited me to sit beside her. Although our communication was very limited, I discovered Bharosha Ma had gained ability to speak a tiny bit of English.

First we spoke of my shawl and we agreed that it was cotton. I had bought it along with a few other shawls to wear to the Rimal's home out of respect. Instantly, because of the many beautiful examples of shawls, saris and sarawl kameez, pant sets, around me, I wondered if it was inappropriate for the gathering, although Bharosha Ma's clothing always seemed to be the most understated when compared to the women who came to the house.

Next Bharosha Ma inquired about the bracelet that I wore; it was thin and crafted of small, colorful faux stones in a faux gold setting. I told her what I could and hoped that she understood me. Within the boundary of the conversation that had been established I mentioned the red bracelets that she always wore. I told her I thought they were simply beautiful. Immediately Bharosha Ma called Tina, her granddaughter, and said something to her in Nepali. Tina left the room and returned with eight of the red bangles. To my utter surprise, Bharosha Ma maneuvered them pass my hand, which was quite a feat, and positioned them on my arm as she instructed Tina to tell me that they were glass. I was extremely grateful and pleased. After that we sat beside each other in silence, her hand upon my arm.

Then softly Bharosha Ma said, "You come to Nepal." She looked deep into my eyes. There was a pause. "You come?"

I felt so full, and in the face of so much love I immediately replied, "I'll come." At the time I did not think a trip to Kathmandu would allow me to do more research for the book. I was not in a place of logic as I sat beside her, the response I gave so quickly came from my heart.

Before bhajans two more noted manifestations occurred. In Hindi, "I love you, Bharosha Ma," appeared on a banana, and the message "I love you, Sujata," surfaced again on a honeydew melon.

Bhajans took place and as usual the men sat on one

side and the women sat on the other. From time to time I looked at Larry to see if he was enjoying the program, and it appeared that he was. I saw him moving his head to the rhythm of the songs, and once I saw him with his eyes closed as if he was truly taking it in.

There were no tears that night, at least not from me. But out of the blue, while someone sang, Sujata gave a soft wail and started crying. I watched her rise to her knees and bow down as she continued to weep. She remained in that position for a short period of time before she regained her composure and rejoined the singing. After bhajans Sujata explained she had seen Sai Baba sitting in his chair. She saw him sitting in the chair that was specially prepared for him.

Did I see him? No. Did anyone else express that they had seen him? Absolutely not. But there is such a thing as clairvoyance, when an individual can see something that others can not. Some explain it as a matter of vibration, that the person with the ability to see is vibrating at a higher frequency and that allows them to experience what is outside of normal human capabilities. I am sure there are people who don't believe that this is possible, but I am one who does.

When the program was over, people milled around, talked and ate. A gentleman who owned an Indian restaurant in downtown Salt Lake provided several dishes for the occasion. Before that, every night, Sujata and Bharosha Ma prepared food for the guests to eat.

Afterwards Larry and I drove home in a virtual silence. Being the kind of personality that I am, Sagittarius to boot, I was chomping at the bit to ask, what he thought about his experience. But I determined I would wait for him to share his feeling. That determination collapsed twenty-five minutes later as we opened the gate to our apartment building. When Larry hadn't said a thing about bhajans, or the manifestations by then, I was very upset. I couldn't believe he could be in the presence of everything that had occurred and not have anything to say.

So, we had quite a... discussion... about it. In the end, basically, Larry said he was still processing what had gone on. Well, that wasn't good enough for the blabbermouth in me. I couldn't understand how anyone could remain quiet under such circumstances. So what did I do? I took a private vow. I vowed never to ask him to attend bhajans again, and no matter what I experienced, I would not tell him. I said I was upset. You see, there I was, sharing something that was having a profound effect on my life with my husband, and he didn't have a mumbling word to say. Vibhuti exploding on pictures. Messages and ohms appearing on fruit. What else did you need to start a discussion? I didn't know, and at that point I refused to find out.

When you consider my silent vow, you can imagine my reaction during a telephone conversation the next morning when Larry asked what time I was going to bhajans that evening.

"I plan to leave around five thirty," I said, as I wondered why he was asking.

“I think I'll go again this evening.”

I wish I could've seen my own face at that moment. "I don't have to leave at five thirty," I hurriedly replied. Larry normally arrived home from work at that time. "I’ll be glad to wait for you."

So we agreed to leave our apartment for bhajans around six. I was happy that Larry had decided to return.

I wanted to share with him what I considered to be one of the most fascinating times of my life.

Later when we were on our way to bhajans, while we were in the underground garage headed toward my car, Larry opened up about what he had experienced the night before.

'There was an apple sitting alone near the front of the altar", he said.

"Yes," I replied. "That apple was a special to Sujata. There was writing on it. It said I love you, Sujata. That's why it was sitting on top."

"Okay." He nodded. "Well, throughout bhajans, no matter how I closed my eyes or looked away, I saw a man sitting in a big chair, wearing a white outfit, with his feet on a footstool... on that apple." Larry had the most confessing, honest look on his face. "I mean, I looked to see if anything was reflecting on the apple; I even looked for a projector, but I didn't see one."

Talk about a bombshell. You could have knocked me over with a feather. I knew there was no way my husband was making it up. "How long did this last?"

"Throughout the singing," he replied. "And when the singing was done, the image went away."

"That was Sai Baba," I said. "You saw Sai Baba on that apple!" I was beside myself. I had ten million questions to ask as we reached the car. "Did I ever tell you anything about Sai Baba sitting with his feet on a footstool?"

He shook his head. "No." Then Larry opened the door and climbed inside.

At that point I began to babble. I repeated how he had seen Sai Baba on the apple. I'm sure I asked another question or two but that may have been overkill for Larry. I felt like he was beginning to shut down and I quietly accepted that.

But inside I continued to play what he said over and over in my mind all the way to bhajans. My husband had been given a private audience of Sai Baba on an apple at the Rimal's house for nearly thirty minutes. That was almost better than my seeing it. Why? Although he is a man of faith, he has a very scientific mind, and I knew he had attended bhajans that night armed with a pure and healthy skepticism.

CHAPTER 9

The following day a group of people arrived from Colorado and the activity around the Rimal's home increased exponentially. It was November 23rd, Sathya Sai Baba's birthday, and the altar overflowed with garlands, flowers, fruit and photographs. That day special ceremonies were held, and I felt deeply touched when Bharosha Ma asked Rameshji to remind me she wanted me to come to her home.

"Bharosha says she wants you to come to our home, and she says she wants you to come," his gaze softened, "and never leave her."

I looked at Bharosha Ma who was smiling, so sweetly, and I touched my heart.

She spoke to Rameshji again in Nepali.

"And of course," he told me, "this invitation includes Larry. After the two of you come to Nepal, then you should travel to India to see Baba."

I nodded as I considered their suggestion.

After that I continued to go to bhajans every evening. Several days after Sai Baba's birthday, a more detailed discussion of my trip to Nepal took place. Sarit, who was a travel agent, conducted the conversation.

"Mom," he said, referring to Bharosha Ma, "says you should travel back to Nepal with her and Rameshji when they return. They will leave the third week of February.

She also wants you to know that you will not be staying in a hotel. You will be a guest in their home. Food, shelter, even clothing will be given to you."

I looked at Bharosha Ma, her eyes were beaming with kindness and excitement, and I was simply amazed by her generosity.

Bharosha Ma spoke to Sujata, and Sujata turned to me.

"Like me, Mommie says you are her daughter." She smiled. "Now we are sisters," Sujata proclaimed.

So many times was my heart moved by the words and actions that took place during the first months of meeting Bharosha Ma.

During a subsequent conversation I asked Sarit for more travel details. How long would I be staying? Two weeks was the suggested time. I would stay in Kathmandu for two weeks, then I would go to Puttaparthi, perhaps have Larry meet me there, and together we would travel home. Sarit informed me I should prepare to have my ticket purchased at the same time as the Adhikari's.

As exciting as the thought of traveling to Kathmandu, Nepal was, I want to explain my mindset. No doubt, I was excited, but there was so much happening around me that even that trip seemed surreal. I was no stranger to traveling outside of the United States, and Larry and I had actually lived in Guangzhou China for one year, but the ride my life was on in Salt Lake City, Utah was shifting my perspective of reality in a way a physical trip could never do. So, to project my thoughts toward what it would be like to stay in Bharosha Ma and Rameshji's home in Kathmandu, a place where I had been told astonishing events had taken place, was more than I could focus on. I imagined what it would be like whenever we spoke of it, but afterwards I let it go.

In my present space, there were so many manifestations, and a plethora of stories from people who were coming to the Rimal's with accounts of fascinating things they had experienced surrounding Sai Baba.

As I write this memoir, I also noticed a shift in my journal notes. I had begun to pick and choose what I documented. Based on some of my entries it appears the purpose of my journal had changed. Was it to keep an account of the phenomenon that surrounded Bharosha Adhikari in order to write a book? Or had I evolved into a startled seeker, a tiny leaf caught in powerful currents, a simple witness to the flow of an eternal river? I believe I can answer yes to both questions, particularly after what happened the next day.

A guest, LaVonne Wells, joined me at the Rimal's that evening. It was a pretty quiet setting after the large birthday celebration crowd. From what I recall, it was simply the Rimals, Bharosha Ma, Rameshji, me and LaVonne. There were several attendees who generally arrived late every night. They had not come yet.

We were in the middle of bhajans when Bharosha Ma physically moved Sujata's head and focused her gaze on a corner curio cabinet sitting to the right of the altar. It was perhaps six or seven feet high and made of glass shelves with glass sides and backing. Inside Sujata displayed brass Hindu gods on one shelf, several angels on another, a nativity like scene with Jesus and Mary on a third, and more angels on a shelf below. They focused on that cabinet as the singing continued.

I must say Bharosha Ma was the most animated. She was pointing and whispering. Finally, I couldn't take it any longer. I had to know what was going on, so I leaned toward Sujata, who sat to my right. "What is it?" I asked. No sooner had I positioned myself as such, when a large human eye, looking directly at us from the back glass panel came into view! It was as clear as my hands are right now, typing on the keys of my computer. I saw a large dark pupil surrounded by ample eyelashes and what appeared to be black eye liner around the rim of the eye! Immediately I jumped back. Startled by what I had seen.

Bharosha Ma looked at me with a knowing smile.

"Did you see it?" Sujata whispered.

"Yes," I replied, still stunned.

"What did you see?" She asked.

"I saw a large eye looking at us. Did you see it?"

"No," Sujata said. "But Mommie said she could see Baba's eyes. That he was watching us sing bhajans."

Bharosha Ma nodded. Then tilted her chin up as if to ask, did you see it?

"I saw an eye," I repeated softly so they both could hear. "Bharosha Ma saw two eyes?" I asked.

"Yes," Sujata said. "She says there were two."

"I only saw one," I said. "But I saw it."

Of course by now everyone wanted to know what was happening, and others tried to see the eye or eyes watching us from the curio cabinet, but the moment had passed.

That happened to me. This time it was not someone else's experience. It was mine and Bharosha Ma's, and it would be told over and over again, like Larry's sighting of Sai Baba on the apple.

Three days later I experienced a unique culmination of events. Rameshji showed me the ring that Sai Baba had manifested for him. Although the image of

Krishna was the same as the image on the man's ring in Paris, the setting of Rameshji's ring was much more elaborate.

The image was protected by a small golden dome decorated with an ohm. It had a tiny, delicate clasp, and Rameshji requested that I open it. This time, unlike Paris, I had an opportunity to study the masterful artwork. Even to my untrained eye it was amazing.

"Was it manifested with the cover?"

"No," he replied. "As you can see there's a tiny piece missing. I didn't want it to be damaged any further, so I had a cover made."

"And there's vibhuti inside," I said.

"Yes, Baba has manifested vibhuti on this ring."

After I had studied it to my satisfaction, Rameshji closed the dome, touched the ring to my forehead, and then touched it to his own. Just for a moment I thought I felt some kind of energy where the ring made contact.

CHAPTER 10

As we sat in the Rimal's living room surrounded by images of Krishna, Radha and the gopis, I felt as if something had reached completion because of my encounter with the ring. Feeling satisfied, I didn't want my conversation with Rameshji to end.

"I understand you're going to be traveling to Tucson, Arizona this weekend," I said.

"Yes, we are. We will visit with Sarit's sister, Sumita. She is a longtime Sai Baba devotee. We received a message on a banana from Baba saying that we should go. The bananas here are like the divine fax in Kathmandu." Rameshji's eyes shone with amusement.

"The divine fax?"

"Yes," he smiled. "That's what we call it. It is a tray filled with tumeric. Baba writes in that tumeric just as he is writing on the bananas here. Can you believe it?"

"I'm simply amazed by all of it," I replied. "What is the story behind the divine fax?"

"Story?"

"How did it start?" I elaborated. "How did it come about?"

"Oh I see." Rameshji paused. "Tumeric began to pour from a photo of Baba."

"Now this is tumeric, the spice?"

"Tumeric is a yellowish orange powder that is used

as a spice, but it is also a powerful medicine. You have seen Bharosha use it during some of the healings."

"Yes, I've noticed that," I said.

"We brought that tumeric with us from Nepal. It manifested there." Rameshji continued. "So, the tumeric was coming from the picture. I decided to gather it up and put it on a plate, put it on the tray. And it sat there for long time. It was in the corner of the room where we hold bhajans, and after a while people were touching it and it was collecting dirt. One day I decided to clean it up. I picked things out of it and wiped it clean with my hand. When I stopped I saw what looked like an ohm in the tumeric but I thought it was due to the motion of my hand, so I wiped it clean again, and the ohm appeared again. I did it a third time and the ohm came back. So." He nodded. "I thought there is something here. And I covered the dish with a protective piece of glass, and put it in a safe area under the statue of Shirdi Baba. The next day when I checked the tumeric there was the symbol for Christianity on it. A cross. The third day when I checked it a circle had appeared, the symbol for Buddhism." Rameshji's brows rose. "The fourth day there was the symbol for Zoroastrianism. And the fifth day the symbol for Islam was there. A crescent and star."

"One religion after another."

"Then there was a personal message for me, 'Ramesh come to Baba.' For awhile messages came every day, and then for several months there was nothing. Now messages come on some days, and on some days there is nothing."

"When did this start, Rameshji?"

"It was back in 1993," he replied.

"That is absolutely... what can I say?"

"It is amazing," he said. "There are many amazing things that surround Bharosha but it is difficult work too."

"I noticed sometimes she looks very tired."

"Yes, she gets tired. Bharosha suffers, but is part of her karma," Rameshji stated. "Because of the high blood pressure and the diabetes, sometimes she gets weak after doing many healings. She has also fainted after doing healings on people with cancer, and her work is not finished even then. Before she goes to bed at night Bharosha recalls all the faces of the people that she has been healing. She thinks of their conditions and she prays for them. Sometimes she does not go to sleep until two in the morning because she is praying for the people that she is healing. So it is not easy work."

I thought of the gentle woman I had come to know. "No it isn't," I replied.

"Many things happen around Bharosha."

"Like what?" I asked.

"Once we were walking down the street, and this rare rudraksha bead fell into Bharosha's hair out of the trees. You know what a rudraksha is?"

"Yes. It's a kind of prayer bead that comes from an evergreen type tree in Nepal. Actually when their strung together they remind me of a rosary."

"They are similar because they are prayer beads," Rameshji replied. "But one of the rarest rudraksha beads has only one partition, one mukhi."

"One face."

"Yes. That kind of rudraksha dropped into Bharosha's hair while we were walking down the street."

"So things just appear for her," I said as Bharosha Ma came in and joined us.

"They do," Rameshji agreed. "Including money. We have been walking and money has appeared on the street at a time when we needed it. Once we boarded a plane leaving the United States with only four dollars in our pocket. Bharosha went to the bathroom and returned with two hundred dollars." His eyes seem to search my face to see if I truly believed what he was saying. "There's more," Rameshji said. "On two occasions, when a certain sum of money was needed, on the day when it was due, I lie in my bed and watched our bedroom door open ever so slightly, and a hand tossed an envelope onto our bed with the exact amount of money that was required." He paused. "Now a mole is coming on Bharosha's cheek in the exact same spot where Baba has a mole." He looked at this wife's face.

Like a young, bashful girl Bharosha Ma turned her left cheek toward me. I could see that a mole was developing where the Avatar has a mole.

"These are the kinds of things that are happening," Rameshji said as Bharosha Ma left the room. "She seems quiet and very normal, but..." He shook his head with a serious look on his face. "She is not. Do you know when and where Bharosha was born?"

"No," I replied.

"She has the same birth date as Swami, as Baba, November 23rd."

My jaw dropped and my mouth opened.

"But Bharosha was born in 1949," Rameshji continued. "Using the Nepali calendar her birth date is called Mansir 10. Sometimes it falls on November 22nd, but she was born on November 23rd."

I found the coincidence of Bharosha Ma having the same birth date as Sai Baba absolutely uncanny.

"Where was she born?" I asked, unable to guess what Rameshji might say, but I was still surprised at his answer.

"She was born where Buddha's palace is located in Taulihawa, Kapilbastu," he replied. "Her family still owns land there."

"And you can see ruins of the actual palace?"

"Yes." He nodded patiently. "You can see ruins. Siddhartha Gautama's mother...he is known as Gautama Buddha or The Buddha... his mother, Maya, was traveling in Lumbini when he was born. But The Buddha spent much of his childhood, literally, a very, very short distance from her birthplace. Lumbini is like the state, while Kapilbastu is the district, and Taulihawa is a town."

"Interesting," I said.

"Yes, it is," Rameshji replied." "When Bharosha was born she was given the name Indira. I gave her the name Bharosha when we married. It is a Hindu tradition for the husband to give his wife a new name."

"I remember hearing something about that," I said before I rushed on. "Tell me. What are Bharosha Ma's parent's names? Does she have any brother and sisters?"

"Bharosha's father is Chinta Mani Gywali, and her mother's name is Lila. They had six children; five girls and one boy. Bharosha is the oldest. Her sisters are Bunu, Anju, Manju and Ranju, and there is one brother, Sunil. He is the youngest."

"So Bharosha Ma was born on Baba's birth date, and near the land where The Buddha was born." I mulled over the new information.

"Siddhartha was born in Lumbini and so was Bharosha."

CHAPTER 11

The unusual was the norm at the Rimal's. The following evening when I arrived was no different.

For convenience sake, before bhajans, the door to the Rimals home remained unlocked. No one was in their puja room when I entered the house, shoeless, which was the custom. Being alone, I took a quiet moment to observe the phenomenon that surrounded me. My gaze rested on the Krishna statue where vibhuti had manifested so profusely from the beginning, and had continued to that very day. There were flowers, and a collection of bananas and apples with ohms, fruit that had been offered but had not been taken home.

Quietly, Sujata entered the room.

"Sai Ram, Gwyn. How are you tonight?"

"I'm fine," I replied.

"Guess what, Gwyn? Last night before I went to bed I asked Baba if he would walk around in my home while we slept. And look." She pointed at three sets of vibhuti footprints on the runner that led up to Sai Baba's footstool and chair. "Swami was here."

The next day Bharosha Ma and Rameshji went to Tucson. I didn't return to bhajans until my birthday, December 8th, which coincided with Bharosha Ma and Rameshji's return to Salt Lake. Rameshji described how the people who came to Sumita Uprety's Tucson home experienced vibhuti and cum cum manifesting on several statues, and for some messages appeared on bananas.

Rameshji said it was also a very trying, but successful healing time for Bharosha Ma. One woman had surgery canceled after they medically determined the operation was no longer needed. He also shared a physical description of how the more serious healings, such as cancer, affected Bharosha Ma's body. One of her hands became swollen, and above that her arm turned black up to her elbow from the toxins she was removing. I must confess, I never witnessed her body react in such a way, but I did not discount it.

When I returned the following day Sujata was somewhat despondent. She felt, despite all her mother was doing, negative things were being said about Bharosha Ma and Rameshji, and she was injured by the hurtful words. This eventually led to a discussion about pedophilia accusations against Sathya Sai Baba.

"We cried, Mommie and me, over the things that were being said about Swami, and soon after that Mommie received a message on the tumeric. Baba told her," Sujata shook her head as she spoke, "not to cry. He said that he was an avatar and negative things would be said no matter what. That it was expected."

I watched Sarit enter the kitchen. It was the first time I had heard about the accusations and I didn't know what to make of them. "Do any of the other revered gurus or spiritual leaders in India say that Sai Baba is an avatar?"

Sarit quickly piped in. "Yes, many of them agree. Paramahansa Yogananda. Ammachi. Sri Aurobindo and Anandamoyi Ma have all said Swami is the highest of avatars. They say it because it is true."

Of course I had no way of knowing if the accusations were true or not, but based on the accumulating experiences surrounding Bharosha Ma and Sai Baba, it was difficult to imagine a being of his status performing such a reprehensible act.

Sujata's mood lightened somewhat as the day progressed. When you think about it, the Rimal's life had been turned inside out by Bharosha Ma's presence. The last time she had visited Salt Lake City was five years prior, and I was told the crowds were much smaller then. Now, partially because of Wake Up Laughing, written by an American, whatever normal life they had, whatever normal routine they enjoyed no longer existed. The telephone rang constantly, and the curious, the needy and the faithful came. All were welcomed without question, and the emotional and physical wear and tear on their home was real. It doesn't matter what high purpose may have brought the people to the Rimal's house, when large numbers of people gather, most of them strangers, mishaps, misunderstandings and misdeeds occur. In such a pressure cooker, I now believe divinely designed, the good and the bad surfaced, individually and collectively.

"Are you feeling any better, Sujata?" I asked a little later as she cut up vegetables for the evening meal and I swept the kitchen floor.

"I'm better. My head hurts." She touched her temple with the back of her hand. "But mostly I'm just tired. I go to work so early. Then I come home and prepare for the devotees." She rested her hand that still held the knife against the kitchen counter. "I'm only a human being, Gwyn, and this is hard work. Sometimes I feel people don't realize how hard."

"Well, maybe you can get Mommie to do a healing on you, to help you get rid of the headache."

She shook her head slowly. "No-o."

"Did you know Bharosha can not use her ability to heal on herself?" Rameshji asked as he entered the room.

"No, I didn't," I replied.

"She can not. Baba is responsible for healing Bharosha. She can not use it for her own benefit," Rameshji explained. "Baba does not heal himself either. The power is not used for their own benefit. So when it comes to family, like most physicians who do not treat their own family members, it is the same with Bharosha. Sometimes a little something here or there but in general...." He shook his head.

I thought about this nuance in Bharosha Ma's healing abilities as Sujata continued her work in the kitchen. I had also noted other differences when it came to Bharosha Ma's family.

At that time there were very few, if any, messages appearing for attendees in general; although I had been shown Hindi messages on bananas for the Rimals, Bharosha Ma and Rameshji. I was told these communications were appearing every day. Bharosha Ma would place one to three bananas in an opening of a cocktail table covered with glass; it served as part of their shrine, and the messages would appear. The writing was so uniformed that it was uncanny. There were bananas that had as many as five lines of Hindi characters on the hull. This method of communication from Sathya Sai Baba, according to Sarit, had garnered the nickname of the banana fax.

On this particular day I arrived at the Rimals early because of a special ceremony. While I was there a message appeared on a banana advising Sujata that devotees were coming. It asked her not to be angry, and to take care of them. The tone of the message got a laugh out all of us, especially Sujata. Minutes later another message appeared on the banana fax but it was written in English! The words I love you were very clear but the name that followed was indiscernible. I looked at it and I had no idea what it was, and at the same time my mind was wrestling with the fact that the message was in English. To my knowledge, that had not occurred before.

As I retell the situation it is very obvious to me, although I had witnessed and seen many things, each time the events took another turn that was out of my normal scope of reality, I was at a loss. It was as if my mind could not adjust fast enough to the reality that was unfolding around me.

It may have been five minutes later when the telephone rang. A man named Lenny was on the line. He was traveling from Arizona with a friend, Rose, and her daughter, Leanna. They were Sai Baba devotees and they were trying to find the Rimal's home. They had witnessed the events in Tucson and had driven to Salt Lake City to be a part of what was taking place there. Directions were given and it was concluded that these were the devotees that Sai Baba had foretold would come. There was another thing that became clear with the phone call; the mystery name on the banana. The message said, 'I love you, Lenne'.

When the devotees arrived Sujata took care of them just as Sai Baba asked by offering food and chai. Leonard Larsen, a kind man, was extremely pleased that a message had appeared on a banana for him. He and I were talking when Bharosha Ma came over and touched a gold medallion of Sai Baba that Lenny wore around his neck. Moments later to our astonishment, the air filled with a wonderful, sweet, floral scent as vibhuti appeared on Lenny's medallion.

"Vibhuti is coming on my medallion," Lenny said, his face bright with joy. "It's coming on my medallion! Oh my! Look at it!" he exclaimed.

Now I had witnessed the entire manifestation, but I still stood there stunned and wondering what had taken place. I can only chock it up to how difficult the mind can be to accept things that are outside of the realm of logic. No doubt I am a person of faith, and my spiritual pursuits have been many, but I've also been someone who has dealt with only facts as a news reporter, and the world I was living in at the Rimal's home was beyond that.

CHAPTER 12

Invitations for Bharosha Ma, with offers of paid tickets arrived from around the country. Some requests even came from Canada, but it became obvious to me, and Rameshji stated it as a fact, that they would not accept any of them unless Sai Baba sanctioned it. Decisions of that magnitude were left up to Baba. This is how Bharosha Ma and Rameshji lived their lives. I was told it had been that way ever since the arrival of the divine fax. They were, according to what I had read on the subject, devotees who had totally surrendered their lives to the guru's will, in this case, the Avatar.

Something else was going on in the Salt Lake City valley. Bharosha Ma had begun to accept invitations to various homes. People with a plethora of needs from illnesses to negative spirits were requesting her presence, as well as those who simply wanted a few bhajans sung in their personal space.

At evening bhajans the following day reports of vibhuti appearing on the objects of worship in these homes accrued. If the primary path of worship was Christianity and the object was a statue of Jesus Christ, vibhuti would appear on that statue. If the believer was a Hindu it would appear on the Hindu god they worshipped, if the believer was Buddhist the manifestation would appear on the objects of their devotion or their practice. The people who gathered at the Rimal's were a reflection of that diversity because Sai Baba encouraged people to continue their faith, even after they had come to know of him.

I was inspired by what I heard and hesitantly asked if Bharosha Ma would come to my home. Sujata told me that she would and a date was set. That day a message arrived from Sai Baba informing Bharosha Ma and Rameshji that they should leave Salt Lake City for Kathmandu after a special Shivaratri celebration, the celebration of Shiva's birthday. I was told that I should prepare to travel with them. Arrangements were made for our tickets to be purchased simultaneously.

I profess I was more than a little excited that Bharosha Ma planned to come to my home. I had no idea what would happen but I did not want to be unprepared. I meticulously cleaned my house and spruced up my prayer space. This caught my husband's attention and with light humor he teased me about it.

The day arrived and Bharosha Ma came. Of course, she was not alone. Rameshji, Sarit, Sujata, Tina and little Maya, the Rimal's niece, accompanied her. Larry and I offered seats to our guests in our living room, and I was secretly nervous, hoping my home, a condo, was presentable.

Once everyone had settled in, I served Indian chai that turned out to be mediocre at best, especially compared to Sujata's, and a homemade apple puff pastry that I think made up for it.

Minutes after the food was served Rameshji said, "Bharosha wants to know if you have a quiet place where she can pray."

"Yes, I do," I eagerly replied. "I have an altar in my

room."

"Take her there," he advised.

Bharosha Ma rose from her seat and followed me into my bedroom. When she saw my bed ripe with several plump pillows, she impetuously lie down and dramatically, but gently, draped the back of her hand across her forehead. I was duly surprised, amused and deeply honored in a most personal way. After her moment of lightness Bharosha Ma stood up and I directed her toward my altar that was hidden behind the shoji screen.

I had several photographs of Sai Baba that Jan and Sarit had given to me, along with other spiritual images. I also had a small flowing, water fountain that lent a gentle sound. With bright eyes Bharosha Ma pointed at the fountain.

"You like my fountain?" I asked and stated at the same time, pleased by her reaction.

She smiled but her countenance changed just that quickly. I could tell she was already preparing for prayer so I left the room.

Conceivably, a minute and a half passed before Bharosha Ma emerged and returned to her seat. Light conversation ensued for perhaps, three minutes before Bharosha Ma said, "I smell."

"She says that," Rameshji announced, "when something has come. Go." He pointed to my bedroom door. "See what is there."

I got up immediately and went to my altar. Vibhuti had manifested on three of Sai Baba's photos. I came out and told everyone what I saw.

"Good," Rameshji said. "That was very quick. Sometimes it takes awhile before it comes. And sometimes we walk through the door and vibhuti and cum

cum simply appear. But this is good. I don't know how to say it, but there is some...." He gestured with his hand. "Some...."

"Some kind of energy," I offered.

"Yes. Some kind of energy here. I think so," he surmised.

We talked for a few minutes more, but my thoughts were on the vibhuti that had appeared on my photos. It was thick and circular like a raised planet set in the midst of an explosion of stars, sprinkles of vibhuti.

Finally Sarit announced, "Gwyn and Larry, it is time for us to go. We must visit another home but thank you for having us."

"Thank you for coming" I reluctantly replied, disappointed that the visit had come to such a quick end.

Bharosha Ma stood up first. She walked directly to me, saying something to Sarit as she advanced. Her gaze pinned me in an unusually probing way.

"Mom says this is how Swami will be looking at you when you are in India."

"Yes," Bharosha Ma said accompanied by a pronounced nod, before she donned the intense look again standing maybe four feet away.

For me the thought of Sai Baba probing me so deeply was just another unexpected element on my overflowing plate of having no idea what to do or think. So I simply watched Bharosha Ma as she walked passed me toward the front door of our unit, before I followed in her footsteps.

Larry and our guests were saying good-bye when once again Bharosha Ma said, "I smell". She pointed behind my head.

I turned and looked up at a small wooden carving

of Radha and Krishna that I had recently acquired. It was sitting on a small decorative shelf mounted on the wall. Now a thick layer of vibhuti nearly covered Krishna and dusted the shelf, but Radha was barely touched.

"Larry," I called, "vibhuti has appeared on this statue."

My husband joined me to see what had occurred.

What happened next is somewhat confusing. For some reason I remained in the living room near Bharosha Ma as she stood at the door. Larry on the other hand, according to him, offered to show the rest of the family the office that we shared. He said he pointed out my computer where I had written my novels, and then his desk. While this occurred I was standing between Bharosha Ma and the Radha Krishna manifestation. This, I believe, is the sequence of the next manifestation. Larry and the others were coming out of the office when once again Bharosha Ma said, "I smell."

In a hurry, I went back into my bedroom to my altar, but I didn't see anything new.

All of a sudden I heard Sujata shout, "Gwyn! Gwyn! You must come see this!"

She was shouting from my office so I rushed to that room.

"Baba has put vibhuti on your computer screen," Sujata said, obviously surprised.

There it was. A splash of vibhuti that resembled a large nebulae was on my empty computer screen!

"This is unique," Rameshji said. "I have never known Baba to bless an object like this. This is quite unique. I think Baba is blessing your work."

Totally astonished I stared at my computer. "There is also vibhuti on these photos," I pointed at a collage of photographs that I had recently assembled of Sai Baba and his parents. Nearly each photograph had a smattering of vibhuti.

"Gwyn, I have never seen anything like this," Sujata said, referring again to the vibhuti that had manifested on my computer.

"What do you make of this, Larry?" Rameshji asked at the height of the moment.

My husband, master of dry wit that he is, replied, "You see it came on her computer. I'm going to start using that one."

We all laughed.

After they left Larry took photographs, and I discovered a small framed picture of Sai Baba that had a small but significant amount of cum cum. I say significant because in a quiet prayer I had asked Sai Baba to manifest the beautiful red cum cum in my home.

Larry and I talked briefly about what had taken place. I could've talked all evening, but as he became more contemplative I decided to go and sit in my prayer space. It was the first opportunity I had to absolutely study manifested vibhuti, and I stared at the grayish ash that clung to the glass. I concluded that it appeared the vibhuti manifested from inside the photograph out, much like a small version of the Big Bang.

No matter what you might think at this point, the investigative reporter in me was still alive and well. So what did I do? I took some vibhuti into my hand that Sujata had given to me before Bharosha Ma arrived, and I attempted to throw it on another photograph. Immediately, the vibhuti powdered the air. It never reached the photo although I sat very close. The other result...my hand was a mess. The natural moisture in my palm was the culprit. It caused the majority of the vibhuti to remain inside my hand.

CHAPTER 13

Just as Bharosha Ma was being invited all around the country, people from all around the country were coming to Salt Lake City. Every day the numbers seem to swell. Sometimes the attendees overflowed into the Rimal's kitchen and into their living room, and once in a while messages would appear for one of them on the banana fax. Niru Bista, a Nepalese woman who lived in the United States part-time, was one of the fortunate ones, with an unfortunate ending.

Niru saw that it was her name coming in on one of the bananas with a message. In her exuberance she reached out and picked it up, and to my amazement, and her dismay, not only did the message stop darkening but the letters began to smear like ink written words on paper doused in water.

Word was spreading that I would be traveling back to Nepal with the Adhikaris and that I was also going to India to see Sai Baba. Interesting tales emerged about trials and tribulations that many encountered in their quest to go and physically see the Avatar. Even more interesting were some of the things people learned about themselves while they were there. Among the growing participants was Dr. Sunny Anand of Arkansas and his family. I had been told Dr. Anand was very fond of Bharosha Ma. It was through Dr. Anand's wife Itti's excellent translation skills that Bharosha Ma warned me that the energy in Puttaparthi was very purifying. She advised me to acknowledge my negative thoughts, but once done I should let them go.

One evening when there was a very large crowd Bharosha Ma sang a bhajan that opened my floodgates again. The entire song was in Hindi, and I did not understand what it was about, but there was something in the way she sang it, something about the melody that moved me, deeply.

That evening, when everyone was socializing after the program, Rameshji approached me for one of our talks. In the course of that I asked him about the bhajan.

"What is the meaning of the bhajan Bharosha Ma sang tonight, Rameshji? As soon as she began to sing it, I began to cry. I cried the entire time. I couldn't help it," I confessed.

"This bhajan means if you will not carry me in your arms God then let me lay at your feet," he replied.

I thought about what he said, but the literal meaning didn't spark anything in me. For some reason, I thought perhaps if I knew what the song meant that I would understand why it made me cry. But knowing the basic message within the song didn't help me understand my reaction at all. Finally, I said, "I don't know what happened to me when I heard Bharosha Ma sing that song."

Rameshji smiled slightly. "Once we were in Puttaparthi and we went in for an interview with Baba. While we were there Baba asked Bharosha to sing. He asked her to sing a bhajan. That was the bhajan that Bharosha sang ...and Baba cried."

"He did?" The thought of the Avatar crying had never occurred to me.

"Yes, he did," Rameshji replied.

I couldn't help but think, what kind of sincerity, what kind of pure heart could sing in such a way that it would cause an avatar to cry. Whatever it was I had felt it, and I had the answer to my question.

"Let me tell you this," Rameshji continued. "On two occasions Baba wrote something very interesting in the tumeric. I have photos of it."

He left and brought back two laminated photographs of the tumeric tray full of writing.

"I think you should take a picture of these for your research." He placed on the photos on top. "This one says," he followed the Hindi words with this finger, "the soul that entered Bharosha's body after she died is Sita, and if you want to question or dispute Bharosha about it," he looked into my eyes, "come talk to me. Meaning come talk to him, Baba."

"Who is Sita?"

"Have you heard of the Ramayana?"

"No," I replied, feeling somewhat inept. "Should I have?"

"It's okay," Rameshji patiently said. "Sita is Rama's wife. Their lives are known about throughout the world because of the Ramayana, an epic that was written a very long time ago but is still talked about and discussed today. Baba says Rama is one of his previous incarnations. Krishna is as well. They are all avatars."

My brow wrinkled as I attempted to understand. It was difficult. What I did understand was the roots of what was unfolding around me were deeper and vaster than I could have anticipated. At that time I determined to find out more about Sita and the Ramayana.

Rameshji switched photographs. "This message

also refers to Bharosha being Sita, and it says 'You are my good friend Sudhama'. Krishna's good childhood friend was named Sudhama. Baba has referred to me in such a way and he has written it here.

"That is who I was in a previous life, and although Baba has said I am a good soul, many years passed in this life before I would acknowledge what was going on in my own home." His expression shifted as if to say, this is simply the truth. "For years, 26 years I ignored the spiritual experiences Bharosha was having in our house. This is the kind of husband that I was. Sometimes bhajans were being held but I refused to go. Why? I did not believe the manifestations were real. Once I got angry and threw a photo of Baba on the floor. I was tired of Bharosha pushing this Sai Baba.

I enjoyed alcohol, and I was busy being successful in Nepal's telecommunications industry until I was fired in 1992. Then one day I had indulged in my normal habit and Bharosha rubbed my hand in some vibhuti that had manifested. I was not impressed and I told her so. The next day we saw vibhuti had appeared on many Sai Baba photographs during the night. But I was still defiant. I told Bharosha it only came on his photos. So what happened? Vibhuti appeared on photos of Shirdi Baba, his first incarnation, and after that the ash continued to come in many places, including my bed cover. Gold dust even appeared on a photo." He paused for emphasis. "And there was also amrit. You know amrit?"

"I've heard of the amrit," I cautiously replied. "It's like the nectar of the gods. But I think when I heard about amrit it was associated with some Greek gods and goddesses."

"Amrit is a very sweet liquid," Rameshji continued,

"much more flavorful than honey. This amrit, this nectar came on the same photo as the gold dust, and there was vibhuti everywhere. On the floor. On our stairs. I could no longer deny something was happening.

So I began to read about Sai Baba. I started my own daily puja to him, and as Bharosha and I did ceremony every day, together, manifestations occurred every day." His gaze brightened. "Later we realized there were three phases to these manifestations. First...vibhuti appeared on the photographs. But it also appeared in other places in the house. Second." He counted off on his fingers. "Several manifestations were happening at the same time. There was vibhuti. Amrit. Tumeric. And the red cum cum. This went on for six months. The last phase involved Bharosha. She would get this smell. Bharosha would smell when the manifestations occurred. You witnessed this in your home."

I nodded, but I was mulling over the last thing Rameshji told me. "So she could smell whenever the powders manifested no matter where they were in your house."

"Yes, she could, and," then he repeated with emphasizes, "and... Bharosha could smell when the objects began to manifest."

"Objects? What kind of objects?"

"For one thing small statues of gods and goddesses have manifested in our home."

The words statues and manifest ripped through my mind before they hit a brick wall.

"It is true," Rameshji insisted. "The first one happened on Shivaratri, when a four faced Shiva lingam appeared." He placed his thumb and his forefinger about two inches apart to exhibit the height. "I was stunned that such a thing could occur, but it was only a short time after that manifested when the room filled with a powerful smell. Bharosha and I knew something else had happened, and we rushed down to our puja room. There, the strangest thing was occurring. We have a chair for Sai Baba in our puja room like Sujata and Sarit have here. Above the seat of that chair we could see this large ball, and there was a yellowish gold triangular object hitting the ball. It was striking it." Rameshji's expression was one of remembering. "We watched this action for perhaps thirty seconds before the room became very dark, and then it filled with what I would call stars before an iron Shiva statue appeared."

"How big was it?" I enquired.

"It is 18 inches tall," he replied. "But that was not all. Finally, a rudraksha rosary manifested around Shiva's neck. This is the kind of thing that began to happen in my home," Rameshji said.

"I don't know how I would handle something like that," I said.

"We did not know what to do," he said. "There was a woman from Bombay who came to our home, Parveg Murghelia, and she told us to pour water on the statue while we chanted the Gayatri mantra. I wanted to do what was right by this gift from Baba, so I followed Parveg Murghelia's advice in a ceremony that I performed. I held the statue in my hand and I began to pour water on it but I was startled when instead of water this white liquid began to flow over everything, my hand and the Shiva. I didn't know what was happening. I thought the statue was melting, but then I realized the water had turned to milk. At least that's what I thought was going on so I attempted to drink." Rameshji swallowed. "As I did so my teeth struck this hard substance and I jumped back because I nearly broke them." His eyes widened. "It was not milk. It was flowing marble. Now not only was I in pain, I was more puzzled than ever by what was going on. That's when I called out to Bharosha to quickly bring a bowl or something to put the statue in. By that time the marble had returned to a milky substance." Rameshji sighed. "All of this was very new to us."

"I can only imagine," I said.

"That was such an event for me." He became silent. "After we cleaned up and installed the Shiva in our puja room, I went upstairs and I wept. It was so much for me." Rameshji paused again.

"I performed that ceremony for sixty-two days, and for sixty-two days that water turned into milk. We fed thousands of people from that milk, and while this was going on the Shiva lingam that had manifested grew. It actually grew another 5 inches or so. Then one day the milk turned into yogurt for me to eat."

"Wow. This is one of the most amazing accounts I have ever heard."

Rameshji smiled, slightly. "After that Bharosha received a message from Baba. She said, 'Baba told me the milk will stop' I was so overwhelmed with the proof of Sai Baba being what he said he was, an avatar, that I pleaded with him. I told Him I had been corrected. That my life had not been going in the right direction and I asked Him to be gentle with me. To show my sincerity I performed a special ceremony, offering 108 flowers as I said 108 names of God. I was astonished when amrit appeared on some of the roses and when some of the flowers jumped on top of the lingam. I mean they literally jumped on top of the lingam before my eyes." He paused for emphasis. "Do you know ceremonial flowers jumped on top of that lingam for four years, everyday during worship. That happened every day. Now it simply happens in the morning when the ceremonial flowers are placed on the altar. Over time the Shiva turned to gold. Not only did it turn to gold, vibhuti manifested on it and hair is growing out of its head."

"Hair???" I blurted.

"Yes. Hair." Rameshji stated emphatically. "It is in my home. You will see it when you come to Nepal."

The image that appeared in my head was ridiculous. I could not imagine what Rameshji was talking about. Perhaps if I had experienced the things I had experienced, including seeing a large human eye observing us during bhajans from a corner curio cabinet in the Rimal's puja room, I might have rejected the possibility all together.

"There's so many things that happen in my home, and that happened around that time. On a ceremonial day for the Holy Mother, a statue of Bhagavati appeared. Durga was silver, six inches tall and covered in cum cum. But she did not appear alone. There were two tiny sandals. *Padukas.* Two tiny silver sandals appeared, and they began to walk back and forth around the statue of Bhagavati, leaving their tiny little footprints in the red cum cum." Rameshji sat back. "This is the life that I have been leading with Bharosha since my eyes have been opened."

CHAPTER 14

That weekend Bharosha Ma, along with Rameshji and Salt Lake resident, Jaspir Batia, journeyed to Atlanta. Before they left I told them a friend of mine, Waheedah, intended to come for a healing. I asked if they would look out for her. They assured me they would.

A day later, Sunday morning, I had a telephone conversation with Waheedah. She had attended bhajans the previous evening at Pavan and Chanda Rai's house where the healings took place.

Her voice vibrated with amazement as she talked of her experience.

"I had no idea there would be so many people," she began. "I could barely find a place to park. There were buses from North Carolina. Alabama. Tennessee. And the house was full."

"Did you get to tell them who you were" I asked.

"I didn't have to," Waheedah replied. "She picked me out of the crowd."

"What happened?"

"Well, I was sitting with a lot of women when Mother Bharosha walked into the room. I had been looking at all the women who came in, trying to guess if one of them was her, because I didn't know what she looked like. But when Mother Bharosha came in, I knew it was her, immediately. Gwyn, she was beautiful, and to me there was a special light about her. I don't know." She paused. "Then I watched her scan the crowd as if she was looking for someone. She stopped when she saw me and she said something to her husband. I couldn't understand what they were saying, of course, but I heard them mention your name a couple of times, so I knew they were saying something about you. The next thing I know I'm putting my photo of Sai Baba on the altar and sitting down front. And that's when the tears started and they wouldn't stop."

"So you cried too? I told you what happened to me."

"I did. It was crazy. It was so embarrassing and no matter what I did I couldn't stop. I don't know, Gwyn. That was something else."

"I know exactly how you feel. It's hard to explain." Silenced filled the telephone line. "Did you enjoy the singing?'

"I did. I did. There was a certain energy that began to build in the room as they sang. I could really feel it. And... because of where I was sitting, I got to see the healings. That was...I don't know what to say about that. Mother Bharosha's arm was turning black. It reminded me of how a dark liquid like blood looks when it's drawn up into a syringe. This blackness was coming up her arm like that."

"So you actually saw her arm turning dark?"

"I sure did," Waheedah replied. "I was sitting close enough to actually see that happening."

"Did I ever tell you that I heard the same thing happened in Arizona?"

"It did? No, you never to-old me that. It happened there too?"

"Yes, that's what I heard."

"Well, I saw this happen with my own eyes. I got an even closer look when I went up for a healing. You know what it looked like?'

"What?" I asked.

"It looked like a growing bruise. It was the bluish black of a bad bruise, and it was coming up her arm. I'm not kidding. You could literally see the poisons that were going into her body."

So once again I was told Bharosha Ma's arm was physically and visibly affected by the healings. This time it was from a friend who I had known for twenty-five years; someone who had absolutely no stake in bolstering the validity of Bharosha Ma's actions.

That night at bhajans in Salt Lake City, it was only the Rimals and me. As in the weeks before Bharosha Ma came, Sujata asked Tina to prepare chai and her conversation centered on her mother.

"In Nepal, Gwyn," she touched my arm, "things are so different. You think there is a lot going on here in my home. In Nepal, Baba comes to Mommie's house and visits with her."

"But I read the only place that Sai Baba has traveled to outside of India is Africa, I said."

"Yes, that is true, Gwyn. But I'm not talking about that kind of travel. Baba appears in Mommie's home at night. He comes and she says they have tea, they talk and she has even cooked for him."

"Really?" I examined her face for signs that she might be teasing, but there were none.

"Yes, he really does. He has been coming for several years now."

"Has Rameshji seen him?"

"No, *Buva* hasn't. Mommie says each time Swami

comes she asks if she can wake him up so that he can have darshan...."

"What is darshan?" I interrupted.

"When an avatar or a divine being allows you to see them," Sujata answered before she continued. "When she asks Swami if *Buva* can have darshan he always tells her, no, it is not time yet. So she does not wake him."

I tried to conceptualize what she was saying. "How does he come, Sujata? I mean...."

"Baba can be in more than one place at a time, Gwyn," she replied matter-of-factly.

"No, I mean, how does he appear to Mommie? Does she wake up and he's there or is she in a kind of dream state?"

"No, she is not dreaming. Mommie says a white light comes and then Baba is there."

"A light? How does...."

This time Sujata interrupted me. "You'll have to ask Mommie. I don't know. Things have been happening around Mommie and Baba since I was a little girl. I don't always ask for the details. You know?" She shrugged slightly. "I am use to it. Mommie has been a devotee of Swami ever since I can remember. My great grandmother was a Shirdi Baba devotee."

"Bharosha's mother's...."

"My mother's grandmother was a Shirdi Baba devotee. He was old and she was very young, but she was his devotee." Sujata hurried on.

"Once when I was a little girl, Gwyn, around five years old, when we still lived with my father's parents; my grandma came home and Mommie was praying to Baba, and my grandmother got very upset. Mommie had a tiny picture of Swami. You know, back then, they didn't have the large photographs of Baba like we have today. So Mommie had a small picture of Baba that she kept on her altar. Her altar was on a shelf. And that day when my grandma saw she was praying to Baba she began to say things like, 'You have that picture of this man in our house. You are praying to him. You love him. It is not a right to have a picture of another man in our house.' I remember she even pulled Mommie's hair and she took Baba's picture and tore it up then threw it down. My mother began to cry, and I remember she said something like Baba I want to worship you but I cannot worship you in this home'." Sujata's voice softened. "'So I will worship you in my heart.' When my mother said that, Gwyn, a spark came on the pieces of the photograph, and it quickly grew into a little fire. It burned up the photograph so quick. It didn't burn anything else but the photograph. I was small, but I remember that. So things have always been happening around my mother and Baba.

But it is different now. Mommie is different from before she died. She laughs with us and talks and everything, but I can feel her energy, there's a lot going on inside of her, Gwyn. Many people depend on her now and although she tries to be like us, she is not.

That is why it hurts her so much when people talk and say she is fake and things like that. My mother would not play with God like that, Gwyn. She is very serious when it comes to Swami, but people don't believe. I have seen vibhuti come from my mother's hands. I have seen amrit come too. Not a lot, but enough that her hands are kind of sticky with it, you know?"

I nodded yes, as I imagined what she was describing.

"But some people in Nepal have not been kind to

my mother and father. Once, Gwyn, I had this dream. I dreamed that Mommie and Buva were going to this house to eat because they had been invited, but in the dream someone had put poison in the food. So I called my mother the next day and told her about the dream, and that day they were actually planning to go to someone's house to eat. They don't go out to eat like that very often. Then after I told them about my dream they did not go. A message came the next day from Swami saying my dream was right.

It has not been easy for my mother or my father now that she has these abilities."

CHAPTER 15

After bhajans that Monday night the Adhikaris returned to Utah. They were obviously tired and wanted to go to bed, but not too tired for Bharosha Ma to ask Rameshji to speak of Waheedah.

The next day there were three messages on bananas from the banana fax. One for Sarit. One for Sujata, and the third was for Bharosha Ma. Basically Sai Baba requested that they have the Shivaratri ceremony at their home. It stated that he liked their house, and that Bharosha Ma should go nowhere else while she was in the United States. Baba said the people should come to her in Salt Lake City, and after Shivaratri, February 17th, they should go back to Nepal.

Ever so often I was kept informed of the preparations that were being made for my trip to Kathmandu. The thoughtfulness never ended. The room that Sujata grew up in was receiving a new paint job and carpet because that's where I would sleep. Sujata told me her younger brother, Prajwol, was the man in charge.

Once while the talk focused on the preparations that were being made for Bharosha Ma's highly anticipated return, the people in Nepal sorely missed her and they were curious about the guest the Adhikaris would bring with them, Bharosha Ma sat beside me and began to peel a banana. As she held the partially peeled fruit in her hand, a tender ohm appeared on the light, creamy meat. With awe I looked at the tiny symbol and into the face of the woman for whom it had manifested. Bharosha Ma responded with a quiet smile. She broke the banana in half and offered one half to me, and from that time on the manifestations involving the banana fax seem to increase.

On January 31st, a group of people from Tucson, Arizona arrived. They included Sumita, Sarit's sister, and four others. Sumita, who had also been to Puttaparthi, warned me about the purification energies at the ashram, and suggested that I familiarize myself with the rules. It was becoming very clear to me that many devotees believed people experienced some of their deepest emotional challenges when they entered the physical space of Sathya Sai Baba.

The following morning a special bhajans was held accompanied by extensive chanting of "Ohm Bhagavan Shri Sathya Sai Baba A Namo". After the ceremony, I actually saw a message coming in on a banana for the first time. The Hindi message was for Sumita's husband, Siddhartha. After that there was a deluge of messages on the banana fax. I stood in the puja room and watched person after person receive a message on the banana fax! Name and all. The majority of them said I love you. Freshly offered bananas would be placed in the space between the glass top and the wooden shelf of the cocktail table and messages would come in Hindi and in English.

One particular woman name Nancy from Tucson, received a very interesting message.

"I had gone to Puttaparthi to see Sai Baba," she told me, "and while I was sitting in the midst of thousands and thousands of people, I mentally asked Baba as he walked by, 'Do you really love all the people, Baba?' Immediately he turned and looked at me. Well, I received my answer in Tucson at Sumita's house. Baba sent a message to me on a banana. It said 'I love all the people'. I received another message right here," she continued to explain. "It also said, I love all the people."

"Where is it?" I asked, because the majority of the people were carrying their bananas with messages on them, sharing them with others.

"It's gone," Nancy replied. "I guess someone has taken it."

Bharosha Ma heard and understood what Nancy said. So she picked up a bunch of bananas that had been offered, broke off one of the bananas, and placed it on the banana fax. Not two minutes later another message appeared. It said, 'I love you all the people, Nancy.' And surprise beyond surprises, my name appeared beside hers beneath the message!

I was stunned. I was so stunned that I had to sit down, and once again, obviously being the emotional woman that I am, tears sprang to my eyes. Bharosha Ma took notice of my emotional state and she came and stood near me. In a comforting gesture she drew me close until my face lie gently against her abdomen. But the moment my mind questioned the validity of what I had experienced, she immediately pulled away.

The banana fax was in high gear that day. At least fourteen individuals received messages during a short period of time that afternoon.

As I stored away the photographs I had taken, I made an observation about the writing on the bananas. Some of the English words and names were spelled in almost phonetic manner. It was as if they were being sent by sound. In Nancy's message the word people was spelled, Pepl. Nancy was spelled...Nonche. And my name, Gwyn, which most people pronounce as Gwen, but my parents determined should be pronounced Gwan, was spelled Gowna. Some time later I asked Sarit about the writing; had he noticed anything.

"I've noticed the majority of it has been in Hindi and there have been a few messages in English. They are also written in Hindi script but the sound is English."

"Written in Hindi script but the sound is English. What do you mean?"

"For example I love you. It is not written like I love you in English, but I love you in Hindi...but it's spelled 'I love you'. Swami writes English in Hindi."

CHAPTER 16

A package I ordered from Jai Sai Ram Books arrived a couple of days later. It contained several photographs of Sai Baba. After speaking to Sujata, and with her encouragement, I drove over to her home in the middle of the day, something I had not done without the purpose being a special ceremony. I knew the demands on the Rimals and Adhikaris was high, and I tried not to put more pressure on them by infringing on the only quiet moments that Bharosha Ma and Rameshji might have during the day. But it was Tina's thirteenth birthday, and I had a small gift for her. At the same time it was an opportunity for me to offer the photographs of Sai Baba on the Rimal's altar.

As I drove to the house I engaged in a conversation with Sai Baba, something I had begun as of late. I spoke to the Avatar as if he were present in the car. I asked for vibhuti on the photographs, and I told him if he sent me a message I would be in heaven.

When I arrived Bharosha Ma and Rameshji were alone. I presented the present for Tina, and Bharosha Ma placed all of my photographs in front of the shrine. After that, we talked for a few minutes before Bharosha Ma excused herself in order to shower. I watched her approach the staircase that led to the upper-level and the bathroom. As she ascended the stairs she stopped, turned and said, "I smell." Bharosha Ma reversed her steps and together we went into the puja room to see what had occurred. There was a generous amount of vibhuti on all of the photographs.

We were barely in the room for thirty seconds before Bharosha Ma said, “message”, and pointed at a banana that was laying in the banana fax. After so many messages, a practice of keeping a fresh banana ready had been adopted.

Sure enough, I could see vestiges of words coming in on the yellow skin. We waited until the writing had darkened to some extent before Bharosha Ma removed it. It said, in English, while a plethora of bananas with messages in Hindi lay on display, ‘I love you Gan Bharosha I love you Sowyme’. I love you Gwyn. Bharosha I love you. Swami. I couldn't have been more pleased and once again, stunned.

As Bharosha Ma left to attend to her personal needs Rameshji turned to me and asked, “Where are we?” His eyes sparkled. “This is heaven.”

“Oh my goodness,” I said. “On my way over here I asked Baba for vibhuti, and I told him if he sent me a message I would be in heaven. And you just said, ‘This is heaven!’ Oh my goodness.”

Rameshji smiled broadly before serious creases formed across his forehead. “I think this is significant.”

“What is?”

“That your name and Bharosha’s name appear on the banana together.”

I looked at the message as I thought about what Rameshji said.

“This has not happened before. I think this is significant,” he repeated. “I think so.”

What did I think of everything that happened that day? I didn't know what to think, but my feelings were clear. I was very grateful for the experience.

I took photographs of the banana and of a vibhuti ohm and birthday message that manifested for Tina. Although in my eagerness, of all the photographs that I have of the events that I have retold in this memoir and I took many, the photos of my banana are out of focus or were taken at an angle where you can not see my name. The notes I kept helped me with the style of writing and the spelling that appeared that day.

Later, when everyone had gathered for bhajans, a touching message arrived for J.B. Singh, who was a Sikh, regarding his mother. He had received many condolences because she had passed away earlier that day, so when a message arrived telling J.B. Singh, 'Do not worry, "your mother is with me."' It astonished all of us, and I hoped gave him a unique sense of comfort.

CHAPTER 17

Larry and I dined that weekend with some friends, Steve Proskauer and Lucia Gardner. During dinner I shared what I had been experiencing with Bharosha Ma over the last two months. It piqued their interests, especially Steve, who is a Zen Buddhist. He told us there was someone who might be interested in receiving a healing from Bharosha Ma, and he asked if I could help. I said I would do what I could, and I waited for a possible call from Steve's contact.

The call came. The next evening I rode to the Rimal's house with Genpo Roshi and a man who had been his friend for thirty years. He was from Albuquerque, New Mexico. Genpo had developed a cancerous tumor in his throat, and decided he would seek treatments from Bharosha Ma that Friday, Saturday and Sunday. But after bhajans and one healing, Bharosha Ma told him that she should perform the healings for seven consecutive days.

The following night Larry accompanied me to bhajans. Genpo and another friend, Mark, who was also his dentist, trailed us to the Rimal's in another vehicle.

A couple of days prior, a message came on the banana fax forecasting the arrival of some New York devotees. That prediction came true that night. Among the New Yorkers was a young girl who had been diagnosed with OCD, obsessive compulsive disorder. The family embarked on the trip to Utah after a man they knew in California, who was living with cancer, told them his cancerous tumor was shrinking after being healed by Bharosha Ma. That evening, while they were at the Rimal's a message came on the banana fax; the young girl had been cured.

It appeared, as a result of Genpo Roshi's position in the Zen Buddhist community and what he had been experiencing at the Rimal's, more Buddhists began to attend bhajans. I was told during one of his talks, Genpo said Bharosha Ma was "the emptiest person he had ever met." I took that to mean like a reed she was hollow, exhibiting no ego. One Buddhist, a woman named, Genshin began to attend bhajans. She was considered to be Genpo's top student.

As the numbers and mix of people continued to increase, there was a new disciplinarian tone in several messages from the banana fax. Sai Baba instructed Sujata to make sure attendees did not touch the vibhuti that continually manifested on a couple of the statues. He said it gave him problems with the flow. He also requested quiet during bhajans and during the healings, and that there should be no more social hour after the ceremony. He wrote people should go home.

This was quite interesting because there were attendees who were very reluctant to leave, which put an even greater strain on what had been an ordinary household. J.B. Singh was put in charge of discipline, and a short talk by Sarit replaced what had become a social hour.

Over the next few days messages continued to manifest for various devotees and Genpo continued his healings. On the sixth day of his attendance, Genpo informed me that he was scheduled for radiation that upcoming Tuesday, but he, his friend, Mark and his wife, Stephanie, who I met that day, had begun to think the tumor was shrinking. The following day Genpo said he was certain the shrinkage was real, although the tumor had not gone away.

My trip to Kathmandu was quickly approaching. After discussing some packing details one evening, I had a short chat with Rameshji.

"So you are coming to our home and you will see many miraculous things there."

"I am looking forward to it, Rameshji."

"We will take good care of you, and you will get to eat Nepalese food every day."

"Well, I always enjoy Sujata and Mommie's cooking," I replied. I had begun to call Bharosha Ma, Mommie as many others were doing. "So I'm sure I'll enjoy the food at your home in Kathmandu."

"How long have you been a vegetarian?" he asked.

"I tried it once before when I was much younger and it didn't last that long, but up until a few weeks ago I was eating a little fish. I haven't had chicken or any other meats for a long time."

"Bharosha and I both liked meat. It is not easy to stop eating it." His expression turned mischievous. "After Baba brought Bharosha back to life, Swami warned her that her body would no longer tolerate meat, that she must keep her body pure, which meant absolutely no meat." Rameshji's eyebrows rose. "But one day Bharosha decided to secretly eat a little meat and she became very sick. But do you know after the sickness passed vibhuti appeared all over her body.

"Really?"

"Yes." He nodded. "She has not eaten meat from that day to this one."

I tried to figure out the reason behind the sequence of events. "Why do you think it made her so sick?"

"I think this situation with Bharosha is very unique," Rameshji replied. "I think when Baba gave her a new life it included a new container, a new body, which was needed to house the divine gifts that he has given her: the ability to heal, how the vibhuti comes, seeing and knowing the things that she does. That is what I think. So in order to keep her body pure she can not eat any flesh.

You see, before Bharosha and I went to Puttaparthi, before she died there, a message came from Baba at our home. It said 'Ramesh, you and Bharosha come. Bring your children. I have to charge Bharosha'." His expression changed as he emphasized the word 'charge'. He sat back a bit. "Then the people said, oh-h, now Swami is calling them. He is going to charge them with the things they have been doing wrong. You see, they thought the things we said were happening around Bharosha were not true, and Baba was going to charge us with the falsehoods. But that was not it. Swami wanted to give Bharosha what he has given her and he could not put such spiritual gifts in an impure container. And you know the rest of the story; what happened in Puttaparthi during that visit." Rameshji paused before he spoke again. "What I know is Bharosha is not the same woman that she was before she died. Although she was a giving person before, now she is much more giving and tolerant. She is always thinking of other people and very loving toward them. And," he emphasized, "the vibhuti always comes in the homes of devotees when she prays. Is she human? Is she divine? That is for you to answer."

CHAPTER 18

Bhajans continued as usual. I had been traveling to, and attending bhajans at the Rimal's house every day for approximately three straight months. By this time my body and my voice began to show some wear and tear. My hips, and especially my knees ached after sitting in the lotus-like position for more than an hour each evening. A position, mind you, that my body was not accustomed to it all. I also developed a cold that seemed to settle in my throat. One that was very obvious during the bhajan that I sang every evening. When I first started singing bhajans at the Rimal's house I was an alto, by now my pitch was more like a baritone.

Every day preparations were being made for Shivaratri, and then a special message arrived concerning the event. Sai Baba said that He would physically attend the celebration. For those of us who did not understand what that meant, a short discussion of Sai Baba taking any form took place. He could be the man who sat no more than ten feet away or the elderly woman with the cane. Any and all could be the Avatar, so being on your best behavior was probably a good idea. I recall looking around the room at the faces, wondering which form he would take, because by now there was little doubt in me that Sai Baba would do just as he said.

The following day Rameshji, Bharosha Ma, Sarit

and Sujata took a trip to Spanish Fort, Utah to the Sri Sri Radha Krishna Temple. When I arrived for bhajans that evening, early enough to partake of the delicious Nepalese dinner that Sujata always had waiting, Sujata shared what happened as we washed dishes.

"We went to the Krishna Temple in Spanish Fort today, Gwyn. Did you know that?"

"I heard something about Spanish Fort being mentioned in a conversation yesterday, but it took place in either Nepali or Hindi so I didn't know what was being said."

"Oh yes. That's why we try to speak as much English as we can around you, Gwyn. We don't want you to feel left out. But of course it is the same for Mommie when it comes to English. She doesn't understand much." Sujata shrugged lightly before she continued. "But yes, that was being discussed. And so we went to the temple today. It is so beautiful, Gwyn. Very, very large building, and it stands out so beautifully when you come up the road and you see it sitting there.

Sarit and I wanted Mommie and Buva to see the temple. It is the biggest Hindu temple in this area and we wanted them to see it. You know? Shivaratri is coming and all. But Mommie didn't want to go." She made a face.

"She didn't? Why?"

"You know, Mommie. She doesn't want to cause any trouble, and she didn't know if the vibhuti would come and how the people would feel about it."

"Oh, I see," I replied. "Did vibhuti come?"

"Yes it did. It came while we were singing bhajans. The man who started the temple, Christopher Warden, invited us to sing, and while we were singing the vibhuti came on the Krishna statue, a very large, beautiful

Krishna. His wife, Christine, was also there.

"Did they know the vibhuti had come in?"

"No, I don't think so," Sujata replied. "We saw it when it came. I don't think they did. But after bhajans my father showed them the vibhuti that had come on the Krishna. And it was very obvious, Gwyn," she injected. "It's a black Krishna, and it was all this gray vibhuti on his face. My father told them they could leave the vibhuti on the Krishna if they liked. It's a blessing from Swami, Gwyn. But I don't think his wife was very pleased...so Mommie wanted to go."

"Mommie wasn't comfortable either, huh?"

"No, Mommie doesn't like confrontations. She's a very peaceful person, so she was ready to go."

"Do you know if they left the vibhuti on the statue?"

I don't think they will. They don't believe in Swami, so... I don't think so," she replied. "But Buva says it's the first time, because of Mommie, that vibhuti has appeared on a statue in a public place."

I looked at Bharosha Ma who was concentrating on removing all of the seeds of a pomegranate and placing them on a plate because her grandson, Sanjay, wouldn't eat it any other way. She did not seem concerned about what had taken place at the Krishna Temple, and although I am sure she was aware of our conversation Bharosha Ma showed no interest in it at all. I had come to see it was simply her way. It wasn't that she didn't acknowledge the manifestations, she simply didn't hold on to them. There was joy for others when the manifestations gave them joy, but other than that there was a humble acceptance of what had become her life.

My cold remained the same as I returned to the

Rimal's house over the next two days, but by that time in my journey with Bharosha Ma I didn't bother to join the line of the people receiving healings. I figured when I compared my cold to people dealing with cancer, and there were several along with a myriad of other conditions, my cold simply didn't deserve the attention. But I was dragging, perhaps the immunizations that I had the day before had something to do with it. On this particular evening as I drove to the house, I told Sai Baba that I needed something special from him that night. Something that would pick me up and give me the energy I needed to continue my daily trek.

When I arrived I was told about a new message from Baba regarding the Shivaratri celebration. On a banana, he instructed that the Ramayana should be reenacted that night, and Sarit announced plans to do just that after bhajans. I knew very little about the Indian classic, but I was quite aware after Rameshji showed me that photograph of the special tumeric message in Kathmandu, that it involved Sita. It was Sita's soul, Sita, Rama's wife, that Sai Baba wrote had entered Bharosha Ma's body after death.

As participants for the play were being recruited by Sujata and Bharosha Ma, Sarit called me to the side.

"Gwyn, I have something for you." He removed some papers from the altar. "Today I bought Mom and Dad's tickets, and here are your tickets to Nepal and to India." As he handed the tickets to me Sarit said, "Something special from Baba."

I laughed. To hear those words come out of Sarit's mouth definitely gave me a lift. He said exactly what I had asked for.

From that evening on, Bharosha Ma insisted that I

say a few words about Baba after Sarit had given his talk. I didn't know why she felt I should, but it seemed as if she knew something about me that I did not know, and I was willing to do what she asked after everything I had experienced. So I spoke of what I had seen, and what I knew about Bharosha Ma and Sai Baba.

CHAPTER 19

The healings continued and the people kept coming. Word that I would be traveling to Kathmandu with Bharosha Ma and Rameshji spread, and many people commented on how lucky I was to be going. Gradually I was beginning to imagine and anticipate the second leg of my journey with Bharosha Ma.

Larry had decided not to travel with me. At that time the demands on his job were too high for him to take time off from work. But in truth I believe we both felt this journey with Bharosha Ma was my journey, and Larry supported me in that, although he endured rumblings from friends and relatives who were concerned about my traveling to the east at a time when the Iraq war had just broken out. What did I think about the possible danger? I thought, if I am truly in the midst of divine acts there is no better protection. I believed that was true, and I was determined to go.

Other physical preparations for my trip had begun. Bharosha Ma and Sujata suggested that I take two very large suitcases to Nepal, but very few clothes because I would be given clothing and everything I needed when I arrived. It was around this topic that I truly saw Bharosha Ma's eyes light up in a carefree way. That was a rare thing indeed. I could tell she enjoyed the thought of sharing so much of her homeland with me, and I loved her that much more for it. The light-hearted conversations about saris, bangles and jewelry were a far escape from disease and pain.

The following day I arrived early for bhajans as had become my habit. By then my palate and my stomach had become very accustomed to Nepalese food. I had also begun to feel very close to the Rimals and the Adhikaris. I looked forward to Sujata and Bharosha Ma preparing food in the kitchen, Tina serving plates, Sarit's hearty chuckle and Sanjay just being Sanjay. The pre-bhajans meals had also become a time when Rameshji shared the daily events with me, and stories about Bharosha Ma in Kathmandu. But this particular day Bharosha Ma was obviously absent from the kitchen.

"Hi, Gwyn," Sujata said as she came down the stairs. "How are you today?"

"I'm pretty good. How about you?"

"This day has been too busy." She began to talk about her job. "We had some special pharmaceuticals to test this morning so I went in very early." She piled rice onto a plate for her father and covered it in yellow dahl. Because Tina nor Bharosha Ma were present; I waited until she added the other vegetables before I took the plate from her and set it on the table in front of Rameshji. " And Gwyn, Mommie fell down twice today."

"Oh, no. Where is she?"

"She is lying down," Sujata replied. "I told her to go to bed and rest. I told her that we can do bhajans without her tonight."

"But...what happened? Did she—"

"She is doing the healings on lots of people with cancer, Gwyn." Sujata cut me off. "And with her high blood pressure and the diabetes her body couldn't take any more. You know, Mommie removes the diseases by taking them into her own body and then she gets rid of it. That's what happens. So she is very weak, Gwyn, and that is why she fell down. So I told her to rest. I told her to stay in the bed."

Sujata had filled my plate with food but I just stood there, thinking about what had happened Bharosha Ma.

"Gwyn, come, have a seat," Rameshji advised. "Your food will soon be cold."

Concerned but not knowing what I could do; I did as he said.

"Bharosha will be fine," Rameshji assured me as he mixed the rice and dahl with practiced fingers. "This has happened before. It is as Sujata says about how Bharosha heals people. It is a paradox of divinity, and it is part of the agreement for getting a new life. Bharosha suffers, yes, but she will be fine. Baba will see to that." He placed some of the food in his mouth. "Your concern for Bharosha is good. Baba says to care for Bharosha is to care for Mother Earth. Baba has said Bharosha is Mother Earth, so we must take care of her."

Bharosha Ma did attend bhajans that night but she looked worn and drawn. Still she smiled, slightly, when I snapped a photo of her; a photo that would be a minute testimony of Bharosha Ma's life.

"Are you okay?" I asked afterwards.

"Okay," she replied softly, but it was obvious she was far from her best.

Word got around that Bharosha Ma had collapsed twice that day, but human nature being what it is, the healing line was no shorter. People wanted, needed healing, and Bharosha Ma obliged. Personally, I never heard or witnessed any indication of complaint from Bharosha

Ma. As a matter of fact, she seemed to distance herself from the crowd that evening; quietly observing, ready with a worn smile whenever I looked her way.

J.B. Singh managed to help clear the house out rather early that night, and I like most others went home, but not before Bharosha Ma mounted the stairs to return to bed.

I thought about Bharosha Ma's life that night and what a challenge it would be for any individual, but yet, at the same time, what a gift. Before I went to bed I said a special prayer for her, although from what I had come to know she already had the grace of an Avatar.

The next time I saw Bharosha Ma, which was the following day, I was amazed. Not only had she recovered but there was a vibrancy about her that I can only call renewal.

"Sai Ram, Mommie," I said, using the common greeting as she met me in the puja room. Sai Ram is actually a prayer invoking Sai Baba's previous incarnation as the avatar Rama.

"Sai Ram, Gwyn." She hugged me with a generous smile.

"You feel better?" I automatically asked, astonished by the youthfulness of her face.

"Ke?" What, she asked not comprehending.

"Better?" I repeated.

"Ye-es." She smiled again. "Better."

I thought of how Bharosha Ma could not use her healing abilities for herself, and how Rameshji said Sai Baba was responsible for Bharosha Ma being healed.

After that day I experienced the renewal of Bharosha Ma several times during the months I spent in her presence.

CHAPTER 20

I had an opportunity to speak to Jan on the telephone the next day. During our talk she expressed concern about a conversation she had with a psychic, who I believe was also a friend. The concern involved Sujata and a photograph.

"I was showing her some pictures that I'd taken at Sujata's," Jan began, "when she focused on Sujata. The next thing I knew she was saying something was wrong with Sujata's throat. Actually," the telephone line went silent for a moment, "she ended up saying Sujata would die in two years if she didn't do something."

"You've got to be kidding."

"No, I'm not. That's what she told me."

I thought about it. I had used psychics before. I knew there were psychics, who rendered little to no accurate information, and then there were Psychics, who were amazingly on target.

"How good is she?" I asked. "I mean, are here predictions usually pretty good?"

"I have to say they are," Jan replied.

"Wow. So what are you going to do?" I asked because it was a touchy situation. "Are you going to tell Sujata what she said?"

"I don't know," Jan replied. "I don't know what I'm going to do."

At the time I don't believe I asked Jan if she knew Bharosha Ma could not heal her own family members. What Jan said was startling, but my confidence level in psychic predictions that included a time frame was not high. Yet, there was something very troubling about this psychic being so direct with a prediction that involved someone's death.

But as my day progressed the prediction was soon forgotten. That night at bhajans another woman associated with the Zen Buddhist community came for a healing. I was told, because of some of her recent spiritual activities, she was dealing with what they called disruptive psychical energies. From time to time her body twitched involuntarily, and she also had a facial tic. When Bharosha Ma sat down beside me I noticed how she looked at the woman. Directly after that she said something to Sujata.

"What did she say?" I asked.

"She said that woman has a...how do you say? A haunt on her."

"You mean an entity." It was a question and a statement.

"Entity?"

"It's similar to a spirit or ghost."

"Yes, yes, something like that," Sujata replied.

In the end, like everyone else who came to be helped, she joined the line. I watched as I had many times as Bharosha Ma placed her hand on the woman's head before she began to mouth an esoteric mantra. It was the same with every person who came before her. She may also have given the woman some manifested tumeric and water that was ready and handy in a small metal cup. I cannot recall. But for certain a combination of Bharosha

Ma's hand being placed on her head or a place of concern, a inaudible prayer/mantra and manifested tumeric was used as it had been for many nights.

People continued to pour in from all parts of the country. Now when I arrived there were cars filling the cul-de-sac. Directives to be particularly mindful not to block the driveways of the Rimal's neighbors had to be given.

The next night, and I say night because it was dark when I arrived, Bharosha Ma met me at the garage door. I was surprised to see her standing at the edge of the building under the eaves. Is she waiting for me? I thought. Quickly I got out of the car and walked toward her.

"Sai Ram, Mommie. What are you doing out here?"

She opened her arms. "Sai Ram, Gwyn. I love you," she said with a sincerity that beamed from her heart through her eyes.

"I love you too, Mommie," I replied.

Together we walked into the house. Sanjay was the first person we saw when we passed through an area that housed a washer and dryer on one side of a short hallway, and a coat room on the other.

Bharosha Ma spoke to her grandson. Sanjay looked up at me, and with a winning smile but the shy manner that only an innocent 10 year old could have, he said, "Mummy wants me to tell you when you return to the States she wants to," he changed the words, "she wishes to return with you." He looked down.

"You can come back with me, Mommie," I said as she looked at me in a way that said he is telling you how I feel.

I walked further into the house and Sujata greeted. She was in the middle of her daily ritual of lighting approximately 15 tea light candles. The candles were lit every day for bhajans.

"Sai Ram, Gwyn."

"Sai Ram, Sujata. How are you?"

"I am fine," she replied. "Gwyn," she finished the last candle. "Come, I want to show you something." She beckoned for me to follow.

We mounted the stairs and entered her bedroom where Sujata removed a ring from a jewelry box.

"You know many years ago, Gwyn, I visited Nepal with Tina and Sanjay. I believed in Baba as I believe in him now, but I was young." Her expression was almost one of embarrassment. "And it was going to be my birthday the next day. So I wanted Baba to give me something. I knew Baba had manifested things for people in my family when they asked for them, so that day I said to Swami, 'Swami I want something for my birthday tomorrow. Give me something for my birthday.'"

"How old were you?"

"Let's see. I am 31 now, so I was about 24 years old. Yes, 24." Sujata continued. "So I placed a little silver dish on the altar, and I said as I stood in Mommie's puja room, "Tomorrow is my birthday, Swami. Give me something for my birthday. When I came back to the puja room the next morning, this was there."

She placed the ring in my hand. I looked into her eyes. "This ring had manifested?"

"No, not the entire ring, but the stone was there. It is onyx. I had it put in a ring."

I examined the stone and the ring. It's beautiful, I replied.

"And another time, Gwyn." Sujata touched my hand. "It was Tina's birthday. She was six years old and we asked Swami for something." Her voice inflected. "The next day there was this tiny diamond in the dish. It was so small and pretty, Gwyn. I also had a ring made for Tina with that diamond."

"A diamond?!" I said as I thought, when you start talking diamonds that's a whole different ball game.

I had heard stories of Sai Baba manifesting rings with diamonds or emeralds. The stories were mind boggling but I had never seen any of the stones, and I had never heard of precious stones manifesting in someone's house.

"So in Nepal Baba has manifested many things of this sort for your family?"

"Oh my God, Gwyn. Yes. All the time. Swami is so sweet." Sujata looked down. "Another time when Tina was still a little girl she drew this picture. On it she wrote, I love you, Baba, but she didn't color it or anything. So she placed it on Mommie's altar in Nepal, and when we came back to look at it, Baba had put a Christian symbol on it. What do you call it?" She answered her own question. "A cross. A cross made of vibhuti. Then the next time, Gwyn, Tina drew another picture and colored it. We put that on the altar. Baba put a cross on that one too, but it had four dots of red cum cum around it. Wasn't that nice? Tina was so happy."

These were the kind of things that most people think could never happen, but Sujata was speaking of them with reverence, an absolute acceptance of a miraculous reality. I was glad Sujata had shown me her ring and told me Tina's stories. The more I was around Bharosha Ma and her family, the more they became comfortable with me, and more accounts of continuous manifestations were given.

After bhajans that night I was told for the first time that Bharosha Ma might go with me to India when I traveled to see Sai Baba. I thought about what that might mean, but as I've told you before, my state of mind was rather. As I think about it now, it felt like I was existing in a kind of bubble. So many amazing things were being shown to me and told to me, that in my natural state I don't know how I would have reacted. But in my protective, mental and emotional bubble, the majority of the time I was essentially a grounded observer who was able to take what was presented, honor it for what it was, and basically let it go when something else replaced it.

It was the only way I was able to deal with this new reality, because I knew these things were real. Sometimes I believe insanity is simply the inability of a person to cope with the removal of the foundation of their reality; a reality that the majority agree to be the norm.

So, I was able to cope with my shifting reality, and accept that reality existed on many levels. The one I was surrounded by at that time was created through the door of Bharosha Ma, and upheld by the Avatar, Sathya Sai Baba.

You may think we were experiencing a kind of collective delusion. We weren't. How can I be so certain? There were various, individual experiences that no one else would have known of, if the individual hadn't talked about them.

The truth is we were all balanced people living an extraordinary experience. Just normal people. If you bumped into one of us on the street and we ended up in a conversation about every day life, it would be like any other conversation. But if right off the bat, we started talking to you about one of the many events that occurred around Bharosha Ma, you would immediately question our sanity. If you decided we were not insane, you would probably determine that we were some of the most gullible people on the planet. You would be wrong.

CHAPTER 21

The crowd began to arrive for Shivaratri, but local participants were chosen to play in the Ramayana. It was also decided that a short Christian play where Jesus cured some lepers, one being me, would be on the program. The night would also include the appearances of other Gods and Goddesses, including Shirdi Sai Baba, Sathya Sai's previous incarnation.

By far the majority of the Ramayana actors and actresses were young Indians, and with their family's assistance, the costumes that were required to make the reenactment a lavish affair came together quite easily. Elaborate saris, intricate head pieces and jewelry were offered as props, and with a cast of approximately 20 people, rehearsals of the basic premise of a scene were set, and the wheels for a highly celebrated Shivaratri where in place.

Wahcedah flew in that Friday, a day before the event, and by the time Maha Shivaratri arrived at least 200 people crammed into the Rimal's house. One of them was an ABC affiliated reporter out of Cleveland, Ohio named Ted Henry. He was a very tall man with an impressive emerald ring that he said Sai Baba had manifested, and given to him in India. It was the first precious stone ring I had ever seen that was reported to have been manifested by the Avatar. Ted was there with his wife,

Jody.

Some time that morning Ted asked if he could do a taped interview with Bharosha Ma and Rameshji. I was told Rameshji's response was, before they agreed to an interview they would have to ask Baba. Although I haven't mentioned the banana fax lately, it was still in operation. Hindi messages had continued to come for the family and a select few attendees.

That same morning Bhajans were sung in earnest. Amerjit Batia played the harmonium, Sanjay and Sarit were on the tablas, and plenty of hand cymbals were dispersed within the crowd.

The session always began with the Om mantra, an introductory prayer that covered a variety of faiths. The Om mantra was followed by the Gayatri Mantra, a bhajan for Ganesha, one for the Guru, and then a song for Mata, the Goddess. Eleven songs would be sung before the ceremony ended with a set of mantras and the traditional closing song, Mangala Aarathi; bidding farewell to Sai Baba who promised that wherever this ceremony was held he would be there.

For lunch, tables were set up in the garage and a copious amount of food was served, courtesy of the owner of the Star of India restaurant. Roti, dahl, basmati rice, curried cauliflower, curried eggplant, and kheer for dessert, are the few that I remember.

I talked to so many people that day. The energy and attitudes were extraordinarily high. It was apparent a festival was at hand.

The play that night went off without a hitch. Not that I can tell you how it looked from the audience point of view. I can't. Some kind of way, being the person that I am, I ended up making sure the female participants were dressed and ready when they made their appearances. So actually throughout the reenactment I remained in the garage, where all the dressing took place, accept for when I made my appearance along with Jan and her husband, Greg. Jan and I were the lepers. Greg was Jesus.

But there was one participant who looked amazingly real. I remember thinking that, for just a split second before he entered the house to give darshan. It was Amerjit who had been transformed into Shirdi Sai Baba. Later that night as we drove to the apartment Waheedah told me something very interesting.

"Everything was so nice. It really was," Waheedah said.

"Well, I'm glad. Although I didn't get to see it, I'm still glad," I replied.

"And I tell you it was something the way Mother Bharosha a hit the floor when the man with the white beard and the white headdress came out. What's his name?"

"Shirdi Baba," I said. "Baba says that was his previous incarnation."

"Yes. Yes. I've seen pictures of him, and the man who played him looked just like him. I mean just like him. And when he came out Mother Bharosha went right over to him, fell to the floor and touched his feet. She held on to them. That made everybody else do it."

"Oh really?"

"Yes. It was something. And I enjoyed seeing her dancing earlier in the evening. She was so joy filled, and it made me see her differently. I really enjoyed all of it."

Once the conversation was over I didn't think anything else about it.

Waheedah and I arrived for bhajans the next evening, and there was Bharosha Ma waiting in the corner of the raised garage door. Once again it was near dark and quite cool, but she was waiting basically outside with wet hair, no shoes and a welcoming smile.

I don't remember who told us the news, but someone in the ample crowd of people who remained from the celebration, informed us that Bharosha Ma said Shirdi Baba had actually entered Amerjit's body, and thereby gave an authentic darshan to the crowd. I thought about what Waheedah said. How Bharosha Ma's reaction to Shirdi Baba was extremely dramatic. She knew it was the real Baba come to give darshan. So, just as Sai Baba promised; he physically attended the celebration, but it was in the form of his previous incarnation.

There was another interesting occurrence the day after Shivaratri. A message came by banana fax for Ted, the reporter. It said, "Love you. Love Bharosha. No interview. Swami."

CHAPTER 22

Two days after Shivaratri a small group of people gathered early in the day at the Rimal's. Since the festival the house was constantly a buzz from morning to night. There was even a man who had come to Utah, from I forget just where, without a place to stay, and for several days he was allowed sleep and eat at the house pro bono. There were constant conversations flowing around subjects like how they heard about Bharosha Ma, India, Sai Baba, their unusual experiences, and people they knew who had experienced inexplicable situations.

Then Waheedah's day of departure arrived and the Rimals and Bharosha Ma gave her a grand send off, feeding her a meal prepared by Bharosha Ma. Talk about tears. Waheedah cried endlessly, even through the meal, and like me when she spoke of it later, she said she had no idea where the tears came from. All she knew was she could not stop crying.

That evening at bhajans it was just a few of us and once it was over I went home. I had never completely recovered from my cold, and may still have been feeling some side effects from the immunizations. My body yearned for rest, but my spirit was riding high, and like someone who had come down from an adrenalin rush I slept extremely hard that night.

I barely entered the Rimal's door the next day before Sujata found me and with unprecedented excitement told me to bring my camera. This time I followed her into Tina's bedroom, which was literally downstairs from the puja room, where she and Sarit had been sleeping because of the number of expected and unexpected guests.

As soon as we entered the bedroom she sat on the bed and made me sit beside her.

"Gwyn, Baba came and did surgery on my neck last night."

Talk about feeling as if I had been hit with something! "He did what?"

"Swami did surgery on my neck," she repeated excitedly. "See." She raised her chin.

In one of the natural folds of Sujata's neck there was a distinct, half of an inch, pinkish, straight slash. It appeared to be a cut that was well on the road to healing but there was no scab.

"That's why I wanted you to bring your camera." She picked it up and handed it to me. "I want you to take a picture of my throat."

"Okay," I replied, still stunned by Sujata's claim.

Quickly, she lay back on the bed. I took two or three photographs. She sat up again.

"I couldn't believe it, Gwyn. At work today I thought that might be what happened. And when I came home a message came, 'I did surgery on Sujata's neck.'

"Really? This is unbelievable." I was trying to make sense of it all. "So how did he do it? I mean…what happened?"

"You know, Gwyn, I have been to see the doctor about my throat. I've been worried because it hurt so bad, and I was worried that I might have cancer or something. We don't have insurance right now. So you know I've been very worried. I've been asking Baba, pleeeez, Baba. Help me, because I've been in a lot of pain."

I wondered if Jan had told Sujata what she told me. "Did Jan say anything to you about a psychic?"

"Psychic?" Sujata looked bewildered.

"Never mind," I said. "Just tell me what happened."

"Well, what happened last night was," she paused to gather her thoughts, "I was falling asleep. So I was like half asleep when I saw Baba's orange robe out of the side of my eyes, and I saw him moving his hand. Then it felt like someone was playing with my neck but...I couldn't open my eyes." Sujata ran her finger lightly over the cut.

"I knew something was going on but I could not open my—Baba was moving scissors.... I don't know what was going on, Gwyn." She looked at me as she attempted to make sense of what had happened to her.

"I could feel someone was cutting me. Someone was squeezing me. Someone was taking out—someone was sewing. But it was like someone was playing with my neck. It was not hurting."

"It wasn't hurting at all?"

"Nothing-nothing, Gwyn. It was not hurting."

Sujata looked straight into my eyes as if to convince me that she was telling the truth.

"Baba was here," she said again. "And I know there were one or two other people, but I do not know who. I don't know... someone was passing something and Baba was doing it. Like doing surgery."

"So they were helping Baba with the surgery?"

"Yes, they were. Gwyn, it was so different. I could see Baba's robe but.... it was like half asleep and half a dream. I don't know how to explain it. I could feel it, but I could not open my eyes, and it was not hurting. Later

I woke up because I had to go to the bathroom, and I felt like there was something on my neck like when you have a paper cut. You know, sort of itchy?"

"Yeah, I know," I said.

"I looked in the mirror and I saw this, and I thought what is it? But I was still very sleepy so I went back to bed. When I got up this morning, Gwyn, I could not move my neck. It was hurting, but it was a different kind of hurting. I couldn't move my head completely but I still went to work. Half way into the day my neck began to really hurt, and I thought, 'Oh my God, maybe Baba has come and done the surgery'. When I got home the message came. I came and did Sujata's surgery."

As we mounted the stairs to leave the bedroom I pondered over the things Sujata had told me, and I thought about the cut on her throat. Had surgery actually been performed on her neck? She absolutely believed it had, and by this time in my journey I did too. But there was a difference. Her belief was as firm as her belief in Bharosha Ma being her physical mother. My belief was as dreamlike as Sujata's explanation of how the surgery occurred.

I thought about the photos I had taken. Suddenly, I was afraid that I had stood too close, or had not focused properly at all. I surely didn't want a repeat of what had happened to the photo of the banana with my and Bharosha Ma's name on it.

For me Sujata's surgery was a special event. I had never heard of such a thing happening before, and in my mind my photos were a kind of proof. But by the time we emerged into the short hall outside the puja room attendees were waiting, and the subject of the surgery blended into the soup of ongoing phenomenon.

That evening after the healings, a devotee from California expressed feelings of guilt over Bharosha Ma taking the illnesses from his body into hers. He was concerned about how it weakened her, and made her sick. I had never told anyone but I felt the same way, and found I had grown more and more reluctant to join the healing line, especially for something small, even though Bharosha Ma's ministrations were believed to be a kind of blessing if there was no illness. Actually, by this time I had stopped joining the healing line all together.

But Sarit like Rameshji took a different view. I think his view was due to some basic Hindu beliefs, and an acceptance of pain and suffering in the larger karmic picture had a lot to do with it. So did Sai Baba.

Sarit responded to the concerned California devotee by telling him about messages sent to Bharosha Ma on two different bananas, on two different days.

"Mom received some messages from Swami," he said. "The first message said, 'Bharosha you are not healing the people well'. The second, 'Bharosha heal the people properly.'

Sarit also mentioned how on another occasion devotees from Canada offered to send tickets for some of the family members to come to Canada. They said Bharosha Ma could do healings, and the family could also experience the Canadian area where the devotees lived. Sarit said the family was seriously considering the trip until Sai Baba sent a message via the banana fax: "I sent you to America to heal the people, not for sight seeing."

Wow. So this world of Bharosha Ma and Sai Baba was increasingly intriguing. In one day I had seen the joy experienced by Sujata in having what, according to the psychic had been cancer, painlessly removed from her throat in the middle of the night. The other side of the coin was strict disciplinarian commands to Bharosha Ma, to disregard the effects the healings had on her body, because it was for the people, and it was her duty.

I thought about Sai Baba, who from what I had read, from the tender age of 16 to 82 years of age, which he is now, had been always surrounded by devotees: 60 plus years of scrutiny, of never being far from many adoring and prying eyes. Why would anyone live like that? I can only see that he absolutely believed it was his duty, and it served a great purpose.

By now with all the stories involving the paparazzi, we know from the calamitous events surrounding celebrities here in America, being watched even part of the time is no fun at all.

That night I had chills and fever when I went to bed. I woke up seeing Sai Baba in his world wide recognized pose of bestowing a blessing; a raised right hand with his palm facing outward. When I awoke Baba's palm was raised and directed toward me. Immediately I broke out in a sweat for the first time that night and my fever broke.

Over the next two days a powerful fragrance of vibhuti surrounded me on two occasions. It filled my car as I waited to have lunch with Lucia outside of a Red Lobster, and the following night it came again as I lie in my bed reviewing some of the things that had occurred since I met Bharosha Ma. When I asked what it meant to smell vibhuti in such a fashion, I was told the scent was a sure sign that Sai Baba was there, although I never physically saw him.

CHAPTER 23

A countdown for Bharosha Ma's departure to Nepal began... our departure to Nepal. Many people in America were unhappy that Bharosha Ma was leaving, but from everything I heard, for the people in Kathmandu, the people who had been a part of Bharosha Ma's journey for years; they were more than ready for her return.

Bharosha Ma and Rameshji's newly married son, Prajwol and his wife, Apurna, had kept the household going, and a woman called Madhavi Siwal, and another, Asha Rai, were the main forces behind the bhajan ceremonies that were held twice a day, everyday, on the Adhikari's property. Bhajans at the Adhikari's had been performed continuously for 18 years as of the writing of this book.

But things had not shut down in Salt Lake City by any stretch. There was such an enigmatic philosophy surrounding Bharosha Ma and Sai Baba. Out of all the healings that I'd witnessed over that three and a half month period, I was still bewildered by how the individual circumstances and outcomes varied.

One particular day Bharosha Ma began healings on a woman who could not speak, but another woman who was partially blind was told she should wait until I brought back a medication that Sai Baba had given to Bharosha Ma, that would heal her eyes. I wondered what was the difference between these individuals? On the surface it was clear Bharosha Ma had never met either woman before their requested healings.

I thought about a report from Arizona involving a woman whose cancerous lump had totally disappeared. But there was another person who had come to Salt Lake for healings and their cancerous growth slowed, but later I discovered Bharosha Ma knew eventually they would not survive. The person did not. I wondered, was it all based on karma?

Karma seemed to be a powerful part of the equation, but I had also heard that grace...Sai Baba's grace, if allowed to flow could make all the difference in the world. So ultimately it appeared, it was up to karma, the actions of the individual in this lifetime and previous lifetimes, spiritually speaking and not, that were major influences, and based on them Sai Baba might step in as he did for Sujata with her surgery, if the collective actions of the individual were meritorious enough.

The next time I arrived for bhajans, once again, Bharosha Ma met me at the garage door with open arms. This time Sujata was not far behind.

"Gwyn!" She greeted me enthusiastically. "Baba was here last night. He came to the puja room where Mommie and me were sleeping.

"What?" I looked at Bharosha Ma who stood beside me. She nodded her head in agreement.

"He sent the message today saying he was here," Sujata added.

'So you saw him?" I directed the question to Sujata.

"No, I didn't. But Mommie did. This is what happened, Gwyn." Her brown eyes widened as she prepared to explain.

"I wanted to sleep with Mommie in the puja room. And you know, Gwyn, how we light the tea light candles before bhajans start?"

"Ye-es."

"Well, the candles burn out after maybe four hours. Right?"

"Four...five at the most," I said.

"Yes. Well, we were sleeping when around 3 or 4 in the morning Mommie says, 'Baba is here!' I opened my eyes, Gwyn, but I am still so sleepy. But I open my eyes and a light came from somewhere, and then all the candles started lighting."

"They started lighting?" I repeated.

"Yes!" A short laugh surfaced. "And there was nothing there," Sujata said.

"I must have looked confused, because I was confused."

"There was no wax in the candles. You know how when you wake up in the morning and there is not even a little wax left in the container?"

"Ohhh. Yes," I replied.

"That's how the candles were, Gwyn." And, she gestured toward the altar. "Baba started burning all of the candles at once. All of them burned for about...maybe a half a minute or a minute. Then the flames were gone."

"They all went out at the same time?"

"Yes, they did. And in my hair, Gwyn, these flowers were wound very tightly." Sujata showed me three chrysanthemums and some rose petals that she had pressed into the pages of her bhajan book. "These rose petals were on my body. On my chest," she clarified.

I looked at Bharosha Ma whose eyes were bright with acknowledgment. It was one of those rare occasions when the expression on her face said, 'See all these things are true'.

Bhajans proceeded as usual, and afterwards I spoke to Genshin. It's funny, Larry and I had met Genshin before, after Larry's raffle ticket won first prize in a Zen Buddhist fund raising event. Genshin was also known as Nancy Gabrysch. This particular night Genshin expressed how she had been troubled by her experiences at the Rimal's house, and had wondered how it could fit into her Buddhist practice.

"I've been coming here for several weeks," she said to me. "And this has been a really interesting time. I've never seen anything like it before."

"I haven't either," I replied. "I've come every night since Bharosha Ma first arrived, and I have to say it's shifted my view of reality."

"I think that's true for many of us. I've been a Buddhist for 20 years, and what I've seen here did not fit neatly into my belief system."

"I can only imagine," I said. "But the truth is, from what I've read and heard, Sai Baba doesn't want anyone to leave any of their belief systems. That's why you have all the different religious items on the altar here. Because according to him, that old saying, something like God has many names but God is one, is the ultimate truth."

"That's interesting, because it was a problem for me until this morning," Genshin replied. Her gaze was steady as she looked into my eyes. "I was meditating and Sai Baba spoke to me. He said, 'I don't want you to leave Zen. I want you to go to the depths of Zen.'"

I leaned back. "Whoooa. Now that's deep."

Her already cheerful face brightened as she laughed. "It is."

CHAPTER 24

Connie Shaw arrived with a group of people from Colorado, and they attended bhajans for a couple of days. As usual, the altar overflowed with flowers and fruit and photographs that devotees had offered, hoping that the ever flowing ohms would appear on the fruit, and vibhuti would appear on the photos. This was such a regular occurrence that by now I paid little attention to who received ohms on their fruit, and who received vibhuti on their photographs.

Because of our seating arrangement I happened to notice when Connie placed a stack of playing card size photographs of Sai Baba on the altar. There may have been a dozen of them. I was sitting beside Bharosha Ma and Connie was sitting right behind us, as the usual preparation of songs and who would be singing them took place. In the middle of the preparations Bharosha Ma said, “I smell," and pointed at Connie’s stack of photographs. Connie rose up and looked at the photos, and I craned my neck to do the same, but there was no vibhuti to be seen. I believe at that point I looked at Bharosha Ma and I said something like, “Mommie, I don't see any vibhuti.”.

Well…I watched as Bharosha Ma stretched her arm out and leaned forward just enough for her hand to touch the stack of photographs. With nimble fingers, and without looking through the stack, she reached into the pile and extracted a photograph that had a substantial ohm made of vibhuti covering the surface. It was such a simple thing to do, but it was amazing.

Bharosha Ma passed the photograph to Connie. Several devotees who were sitting nearby also looked at it. It was the second vibhuti ohm, to my knowledge, that had appeared on the altar. The first, of the same size, was the ohm that appeared in a silver dish for Tina's 13th birthday.

That evening was full of surprises, including an account by a gentleman by the name of Reverend Pipes, a Baptist minister who led the first group of African-Americans to visit Sai Baba at Puttaparthi in 1979. There were 15 of them. One couple, Shalaine and Kelly, who were apart of that group, were also in the crowd when Reverend Pipes told his story.

"I was dealing with a lot of trouble," he said. "And I began to call on Sai Baba. He had manifested this necklace for me with a medallion of Jesus. At the time I had asked for one with him on it, but Sai Baba said people wouldn't understand or be able to accept that, so he made one with Jesus on it, acknowledging that God is one. And I had been told, like so many people who've received these gifts from Sai Baba, rings and necklaces and things of that nature, that whenever we were in trouble that he would know it and we could call on him. Well I was calling on him, and I called Sai Baba, and I called Sai Baba. I called Sai Baba so long, I don't know how long, when all of a sudden this movie screen just rolled down in front of me. I'm talking about one of those old-fashioned kind that you would have seen at school back in the day, and they would focus the projector on it, that kind of movie screen. It rolled down, and in the beginning this dot appeared in the middle, and it quickly grew to be Sai Baba, and he walked out of the movie screen. He walked out of that screen, and he put his hand on his hip and leaned toward me and said. 'What is it Pipes?'"

"I began to tell him everything that was wrong, and what had happened, and after I was done laying out my troubles, Baba said. 'I know.' And he turned around, and he walked back into that movie screen. He disappeared. The movie screen rolled up, and it disappeared."

I was laughing by the time Reverend Pipes sat down. The account he told and the way he told it was hilarious. But my laughter was also... what did I just hear? Did I hear this man say, this minister say, there was a movie screen, an actual movie screen...that rolled down out of thin air in front of him and Sai Baba walked out of it?

After hearing another "sermon" from Reverend Pipes the following day called "Hot in the Oven," I basically understood this: Sai Baba physically came to him just to tell him that he knew about his woes, but Reverend Pipes was the cause of his own troubles...so deal with it!

It has taken me years...years, going over that story in my mind and asking my husband, Larry, did he hear the same thing, which he says he did, to accept that Reverend Pipes did not say he was dreaming, that this actually happened to him.

Activities continued to accelerate around our departure for Kathmandu. One day, and what felt like out of the blue, Sarit told me that Genshin would also be traveling to Nepal. He said he was uncertain if he would be able to acquire a ticket that would put Genshin on the same flights that we had already procured, but efforts were being made. I was a bit surprised to hear it, but I truly welcomed her. From the little that I knew about Genshin I liked her, and I felt we would be great travel companions as we continued on to India together. Her travel plans stayed up in the air over the next 24 hours. When I spoke to Sarit again, he had managed to acquire a ticket for Genshin on the same plane as Rameshji, Bharosha Ma and me.

CHAPTER 25

"Everything's set, Sarit said. You and Nancy will spend 3 weeks in Nepal before you travel together to Bangalore where Baba will be at Whitefield. That's the name of the ashram. Are you excited?"

"I am excited," I said, but I also felt like the leaf caught in the current of the river. I would be traveling to Bangalore to see the Avatar at Whitefield, not Puttaparthi.

"You ought to be," Sarit replied with a wide smile. "You'll get to spend plenty of time with Mom in Kathmandu before traveling to India, and she's got lots of plans for you while you're there."

"I know. She's had Sujata tell me some of the things she wants to do, and about some of the things she wants to give me. It's amazing."

"Mom is amazing," Sarit said in a very serious tone. "You know, Gwyn, at first Mom declined being a healer, and Swami told her it was her duty."

"Yes, I've heard that before."

"It's true. But since then there have been times that Baba has appeared to Mom. He has taken her places and given her powers and wisdom."

"Taken her places?" I heard the powers and wisdom part, but I was most surprised and baffled by that part of his statement.

"Ye-es." He gave one emphatic nod.

"Where? Tell me."

Sarit looked down before he looked into my face again. "There are places like heaven and earth, and people talk about the universe and how vast it is."

"Oka-ay."

"Well, there are 14 other places that people...beings inhabit outside of earth."

"You are referring to *lokas*." I needed it to be clear because I knew loka was a Hindi term, and in my mind loka meant realm or dimension.

"Yes," Sarit replied. "Mom has shared this with me and now I am sharing it with you. Mom says Swami has come and taken her to those 14 places. And...."

He paused, so I waited for something that could be even more of a bombshell.

'He took her there in a golden chariot."

Sarit's expression acknowledged how fairytale-like his words were, but I knew he was serious. A chariot. Now I was being stretched that's for sure. All I could do was think of the old gospel spiritual, the song, 'Swing Lo Sweet Chariot'.

"She told me this in private," he said, "because Mom knows people would not believe her even with all the miracles that happen around her."

"That's probably true," I replied.

"But you know Mom; how she says things rather quietly."

"Yes, I know exactly what you're talking about."

"She doesn't say a lot, and they are many things I'm sure I don't know because Mom doesn't share it. She doesn't share because people wouldn't believe her. Now, she and Sujata have a special relationship, and she tells

Sujata things, but I'm sure there are also things that Sujata does not know. Of course there's no documentation of what I just told you, but there is something that was documented."

"Okay." My head was buzzing with what I had just heard, but it calmed a bit when I heard the word documentation.

"Mom woke up one morning in Nepal and they had bhajans as usual. During bhajans Mom said in her quiet way, 'I went to Rishikesh and Haridwar with Baba last night'."

"She went where? Are these places here on earth?"

"They are cities in India," Sarit replied. "They are a part of the Char Dham pilgrimage destinations. Char Dham means four abodes of God. They are holy places. Badrinath. Jagannath Puri. Rameshwaram. Dwarka. Swami took Mom there to all four places."

"Oh-h." This has taken a different twist, I thought before Sarit continued.

"Now, after living with miracles day in and day out, most of the people in Nepal are comfortable with Mom. But still they didn't believe her when she told them Baba had taken her to these places. It's amazing how people don't believe Mom." He chuckled a bit. "She was trying to share this and no one believed her. Well a few minutes later, Swami wrote a message on the tumeric. It said, 'I came last night to Bharosha's home and I took her to Rishikesh and Haridwar." He really chuckled this time. "Then everybody believed her. And I believe there have been other trips too," he said with a broad smile, "but this is one that was documented by Swami's message on the tumeric."

"The truth is these things aren't easy to believe,

Sarit," I replied. "But like you said, people who've been living with the miracles, that are around her day in and day out, you would think that they would be more open to totally accepting what Bharosha Ma has to say." I paused. "So you can imagine how people who have never seen any of the miracles, perhaps never heard of Sai Baba, and they hear of something like this." I shook my head. "They simply won't believe it. It's difficult for me, but I've seen and experienced so much over the last few months that I can't close the door on it."

"I know," Sarit replied. "It is difficult even for people who have been around Mom for years." He clasped his hands. "Listen. There is this man in Nepal named Sudip, who is a Baba devotee. He comes to bhajans all the time now, but in the beginning he was an alcoholic and a drug addict, and his family, who came quite often to Mom's, wanted her to help him. So Sudip started coming to bhajans and receiving healings. Eventually, he stopped all of his bad habits and he became a good man, just a normal person, and he got married, and like I said, he came to bhajans all the time. But even after being helped by Mom, in his mind and in his heart he could not convince himself of who Mom was. He always had a nagging doubt. He would think okay, everybody comes to Bharosha's house and all the miracles are happening and Baba's messages are coming, but who is this? Who is she? It was going through his mind every day. Who is she? In other words, he was wondering what her identity was. Okay?"

"Yes, I understand," I replied.

"Now you know how Swami invites Mom to go to Puttaparthi?"

"Yes, I've heard."

"Okay. A message comes and says come to

Puttaparthi, and like on many occasions, a group of them went with Mom. Sudip was a part of that group. One morning when they were sitting in darshan, Swami came in and gave darshan. He took letters from devotees, manifested vibhuti, and walked around so everyone could see him. Then Swami went and sat in his chair like he always does. Sudip was there in the front row and he was just looking at Swami, and all of a sudden Swami became Mom."

"He became Mommie?"

"What I am trying to say is," Sarit explained. "He was looking at Baba's form but that form changed to Bharosha. Sudip couldn't believe his eyes. He tried to pinch himself. He tried to slap himself because he thought he was dreaming or something. But lo and behold there was Mom sitting in the place of Baba."

"Oh my goodness," I said as I thought this was a different kind of pill to swallow.

"But that's not all," Sarit said. "After darshan Sudip sought Mom out and he started crying. He told everybody what was happening to him because they were wondering what was wrong, because he was acting a little weird. Sudip told them, this is what had been going on in my mind, and this is what happened; how Swami had removed his doubt and showed him who Mom really was. But then again," Sarit made an expression, "no one really believed him."

"So they came back to Nepal, and after a few days in Kathmandu Baba wrote a message. Basically it said, you all have come and everybody was blessed. I was so happy to see you. Pray every day for me and I'll take care of you know, that kind of thing. And then at the end, it said, and by the way, I gave revelation to Sudip about who Bharosha is.

Sarit looked into my eyes. "I get a chill from telling you that even now."

"I've got a chill from hearing it," I replied.

I wonder now why I didn't ask Sarit about Baba saying on another tumeric message that the soul that inhabited Bharosha's body was Sita. I had also heard Rameshji say on several occasions that Baba said Bharosha Ma was Mother Earth. The truth is I don't know if Sarit would have been able to answer my question, but it has become clear to me that the flame that entered Bharosha Ma's body from Sai Baba's mouth when she was still clinically dead was what I believe to be a powerful portion of himself. I mean, Sai Baba is an Avatar, and he espouses that all of us are God. He says the difference between him and you and me is that He knows He's God, and we don't. So I believe that a greater knowledge of the God self, a much more aware portion of the God self was placed into Bharosha Ma's body, perhaps through the vehicle of Sita's soul. In other words there is a greater consciousness of divinity. There is a oneness with Sai Baba, that is why the miracles and events that unfold around her flow with such ease.

But of course that's the way I see it now that I'm writing this memoir. My hypothesis has also formed after Rameshji told me, now it is a common occurrence for Nepalese devotees to see Sai Baba transform into Bharosha Ma after they have traveled with Bharosha Ma to India to experience the Avatar.

But at the time that I was introduced to this concept, I was simply floating from one unworldly happening to another. I didn't understand the depths of what was going on, and I don't know if I had the capacity to understand it.

CHAPTER 26

On the morning of our departure, Larry, Genshin and I trailed the Rimals and the Adhikaris to the airport. I knew I had Larry's full support in my decision to make the trip, although he may have harbored some concern about my safety. The war against Iraq was only 7 days old, and we'd heard that anti-American sentiment was growing in the East, although my travels would not take me to the most volatile Middle East. Despite that, Larry's good friend, George, had gone so far as to jokingly tell Larry he should have hand cuffed me to the bed to keep me from going. But I had determined if God wanted me to die on a trip to find out more about God, then there was absolutely nothing I could do about it.

On the other hand, Genshin, who hobbled to our car when we picked her up because she had badly injured her big toe the day before, faced some opposition from higher ups in the Zen Buddhist community. It appeared they could not reconcile Genshin's Zen beliefs and practice with a highly influenced Hindu trip to Nepal and India.

Several of the people who I had come to know during Bharosha Ma's stay in Salt Lake City met us at the airport. One in particular, a young girl around the age of 12, Herjit Partola, was in the crowd. She had become quite special to me. Her youth and enthusiasm inspired me many a bhajan night when my voice and my knees wanted to fail.

After quite a display of shuffling articles from one large suitcase to another in order to meet weight regulations; we said good-bye to all our well-wishers at the security check point, and Rameshji, Bharosha Ma, Genshin and I began the first leg of our international journey. We took a flight from Salt Lake to the Los Angeles International Airport, where we were later scheduled to fly Thai Airlines out of the country.

When we arrived at LAX, I was surprised when nearly 30 people greeted us after we deplaned. In order not to block the flow of passengers behind us we walked to another area as the enthusiastic crowd gathered around Bharosha Ma. Seconds later I realized I recognized one of them. It was Reverend Pipes. He was carrying a photograph of Sai Baba while a few of the others presented bunches of bananas. In the midst of the frenzied welcome, as some of the Indian devotees greeted Bharosha Ma with folded hands and respectful nods, ohms appeared on bananas and vibhuti manifested on Reverend Pipes's photo. In fact, our group created quite a commotion, to the degree that two travelers and an airport employee joined the crowd and asked Bharosha Ma for her blessing. Genshin and I stood back while Rameshji watched over the crowd, and when it was time the LA group said good-bye to us at security.

During the flight from Los Angeles to Bangkok I sat on one side of Bharosha Ma while Rameshji sat on the other. We slept most of the time, and I marveled at how Bharosha Ma sat in the traditional lotus style on top of the airplane seat the majority of the trip. Later I discovered that Bharosha Ma found my arched travel pillow that wrapped halfway around my neck quite the conversation piece.

There was a short hotel stay, perhaps six to eight hours, at a hotel inside the Bangkok airport. After that we boarded our last flight to Nepal. On the plane and in the Thai airport I ate vegetarian dishes that made me long for Bharosha Ma and Sujata's cooking.

We arrived in Kathmandu, and from the moment we stepped into the small building Bharosha Ma was welcomed with bouquets of flowers, and we were all welcomed with floral garlands and special care. From the photographs for our visas, to our luggage being taken from the building to waiting vehicles, there was nothing we had to think about. But I must confess it is all somewhat of a blur now. There were so many new faces, but I believe that it was in the airport that I set eyes on Bharosha Ma's daughters, Siru and Lily, her son, Prajwol, and Siru's husband, Mohan Charya, who worked for the airport, for the first time.

Once our airport business was behind us, the entire group; there may have been a dozen of us, climbed into waiting vehicles and began the drive to Rameshji's and Bharosha Ma's.

The route to their home appeared to take us through some outskirts of the city. My first thoughts of Kathmandu took me back several years to when Larry and I lived in Guangzhou, China, from 1997-1998. I was back in the East. It was not the West, and I had not expected it to be. There were people walking on dusty roads, creative three wheeled vehicles, heaps of trash, a child being bathed under a faucet near the edge of the street, buildings that looked like they had been there for long, long time, and traffic that only God himself knew who was going to do what. And there were also women in beautiful colored saris, colorful buildings that sprang to life with writing so fanciful that it was art, sounds and smells of a vibrant life, and people with faces from countries and places that I had only dreamed of seeing.

By the time we arrived at the Adhikari's, approximately 50 people were waiting. The welcome flowed from the street, up a short stairway and through a gate nestled inside a stone wall surrounding their home. Eager faces lined the walkway and gathered around four chairs, just outside the front door, that had been prepared for us.

The reception ceremony began with the pressing of a mixture of cum cum and rice against our foreheads. Afterwards we were each offered a bite of banana and yogurt, and then the step was repeated. We watched as special ministrations were given to Bharosha Ma and Rameshji. A traditional type of garland made of *dubo*, a grass symbolic of longevity and everlasting life, was placed around their necks along with other floral garlands. In the end Bharosha Ma's feet were washed, adorned and kissed.

When the ceremony was over, and we were going into the house, the person who seemed to spearhead the ceremony, Madhavi, a petite woman with eyes that exuded sincerity said, "Ohms came on the bananas when you arrived at the airport."

As I write this now, after reading it in my journal, it never fails to amaze me how much I have forgotten, and how grateful I am for the few notes that I took.

Genshin and I added our shoes to a collection of footwear that sat outside a screened door. As we were ushered inside the house there was a door to my left, and another on my right, that opened into what I came to know as the main bhajan hall. As we progressed down a hallway toward a staircase, there was another door on the left and a bathroom in front of us, as well as several photographs on the wall. Among them, a solitary photo of Sai Baba, and another photo that was of particular interest to me. It was a photograph of a younger Bharosha Ma. She wore an enigmatic smile as she sat a few yards in front of what appeared to be a rural structure.

We climbed a stone stairway to the second floor, passed another bedroom and bathroom before we reached our room. It was freshly painted and carpeted as Sujata said it would be, and our wooden beds, which had drawers and storage space built into the frame, formed a L, as they lay tucked beneath open windows that welcomed sunshine and fresh air. A modern day chifferobe provided closet space, and a photograph Sai Baba graced one of the walls.

That first afternoon was a time of rest, and we experienced tea served by Gita for the first time. She was a young girl around 12 who the Adhikaris sent to school and took care of, and in exchange she helped around the house.

Later that evening we attended bhajans with perhaps 60 others. The shrine itself was an enormous collection of religious objects. From small polished brass statues of Radha and Krishna to a large, decorative Shirdi Baba enshrined on a chair. The Adhikaris altar was a feast for the eyes. Various photographs of Sai Baba as well as other gods and goddesses adorned the walls behind and on both sides of it. One huge photograph of Sai Baba was virtually covered in vibhuti, something I was told, had been manifesting for years. There were live flowers and garlands as well as faux ones.

My first experience of bhajans in the main bhajan hall was sensory and sentimental. I was in Kathmandu. I was sitting in front of the altar that I had heard so much about over that last four months, and I was hearing the voices of the Nepalese people who had sung bhajans with Bharosha Ma and Rameshji for many years. I was so pleased to be able to sing along. Many of them had experienced things with Bharosha Ma and Sai Baba that were deeply engraved in their hearts. Some of the experiences I would come to know during my three-week stay in Nepal. But as I sat there for the first time, I was like a sponge that wanted to take in everything.

The singing was done, and the waving of the customary aarthi flame was performed. At the appropriate moment Bharosha Ma took the fire outside to be extinguished, and I was encouraged to join a procession of maybe fifteen women who proceeded outside through a rear door of the bhajan hall. What we were doing and where we were going, I had no idea, but we ended up at a Goddess Temple. The petite building sat perhaps 50 feet away from the main bhajan hall, and housed large, intricately decorated statues of Lakshmi, the Goddess of wealth and prosperity, Durga, the Divine Mother, and Saraswati, the Goddess of speech, music and learning. There was also an adorned Gayatri statuette. A ritual was performed and several mantras sung before a brass bell hanging from the roof of the temple was rung by one of the participants.

Before I re-entered the main bhajan hall I stopped and read a colorful plaque that hung outside the rear door. It was crowned by the five main religious symbols and a border and letters of royal blue. It read:

> Let the different faiths exist. Let them flourish. Let the glory of God be sung in all the languages and a variety of tunes. That should be the ideal. Respect the differences between the faiths and recognize them as valid so far as they do not extinguish the flame of unity. I have not come to speak on behalf of any particular religion. I have not come on a mission of publicity for any sect, creed or cause. Nor have I come to collect followers for any doctrine. I have come to tell you of this universal unitary faith, this path of love, this duty of love, this obligation to love.
>
> The totality of divine energy has come unto humanity as Sathya Sai – to go to each and everyone, to wake up the slumbering divinity of every human being. Even if in your sleepiness or in your weakness for sleep, you growl, grumble or groan, kick, criticize, quarrel or cry. I will not forsake you. I will not let your divinity go to sleep. A mother never forsakes the child she carries or lets the child fall down even if the child works out its resentment and anger on her. I have come to help, to accompany and to carry you. I can never forsake you. I will never fail in my duty to my children and I shall be very grateful to each of mine who helps my tasks....
>
> Wake up my children, wake up to the dawn of knowledge, wake up to your divine duties, wake up to your divine rights, and wake up to your divine reality.
>
> \- Sathya Sai

Baba.

When I stepped inside with cum-cum on my third eye, evidence of my prayers in the Goddess Temple, I noticed, unlike America, the healing line was much shorter. It consisted of approximately fifteen people. I was later told when word first spread about Bharosha Ma the numbers were similar to America, but now the novelty and curiosity had worn off. Now only the people who were sincerely seeking help, and those whose medical options had been terminated sought out Bharosha Ma.

When I was inside the bhajan hall several devotees came by and welcomed me as I studied the items hanging on the rear walls. There were only a few, but one was very intriguing. It was a framed copy of Bharosha Ma's discharge summary from Sri Sathya Sai Institute of Higher Medical Sciences in Puttaparthi. For me, the most interesting words amongst a plethora of medical terms were three observations that I understood. No pulse. No blood pressure. Cold clammy skin.

That night Nancy and I went to bed at a somewhat early hour, and were awakened bright and early the next morning by Gita serving tea. It was a service I would enjoy until the day I left.

CHAPTER 27

Breakfast, as all the meals we would enjoy while we were in Kathmandu, was served in a large kitchen on the first floor. Glass enclosed shelves with a variety of cooking utensils, plates and other culinary equipment could be viewed from a heavy wooden table that could easily seat eight. A gas range and a preparation counter expanded the entire rear wall; while a small refrigerator took up much less space not far away. A side door opened onto a small convenient, multipurpose room with a sink. From there you could descend a stairway that led to the courtyard below. The Adhikaris made a wise use of space, because approximately 10 feet away was the outer wall surrounding the Goddess Temple. It was topped by at least 50 small brass bowls containing mustard oil and a natural cotton wick; in other words 50 outdoor candles.

That first morning, to make us feel more at home, we were served an English breakfast of toast, eggs with onion and tomato, tea and jam. Rameshji joined us most mornings and continued to be a rich source of information. That day he talked about how different Bharosha Ma was from before the resurrection, and he promised to take us on a tour of the property after bhajans.

While we finished breakfast, Madhavi, a retired schoolteacher but also an artist, arrived early for bhajans which commenced at 9:30 every morning. She was excited that vibhuti had already appeared on one of her paintings that she had placed in the main bhajan hall. It was a painting of baby Krishna. I fell in love with the piece when I saw it, and I made arrangements to buy it so I could take it back to America.

After bhajans, when the crowd had thinned considerably, Rameshji told us the history of some of the objects on the altar.

"This is the Shiva statue I told you about that materialized." He looked at me. The one that I poured the water on and it turned into milk."

"Yes, I remember," I said before Rameshji gave an abbreviated version of the story for Nancy's benefit.

"And you see," he placed his hand near a very fine group of long hairs extending the statue's head, "this is hair! It is actually growing."

I stared at the object that was nearly covered in a pile of vibhuti. But the hair, although fine was there, extending downward from both sides of the statues head.

"As you can see," Rameshji continued, "it is gold. This statue was not gold in the beginning. It was black like iron when it first materialized more than six years ago. He pointed toward another statuette. Butter came from this Krishna's mouth and we fed lots of people with it."

I looked at the beautifully adorned Krishna and thought it was just as beautiful as the one in Sujata and Sarit's home, although this one had a very different story to tell.

'Here is the Shiva lingam that every morning a flower jumps on top of it after it has been worshiped with fresh flowers."

"I noticed a small flower on top of a tiny perch

which looked like a short column with a four carved faces at its base. The column, which was the lingam, fit into a carved yoni. The entire Shiva lingam sat upon a wider base.

"And this materialized as well?" I asked.

"Yes, it did," Rameshji replied.

After that my attention strayed to several rectangular containers behind the altar. Piles of the cum cum and tumeric, along with some coconuts were inside each one.

"Is this where you keep the cum cum and tumeric that is used? Like the tumeric Bharosha Ma uses for healing?" I asked.

"Yes, it is kept here," Rameshji replied. "They have been manifesting the powders continuously for years."

"Manifesting?" I repeated as I took a closer look.

"Yes. They are coming from the photos. From the photographs."

It was only then that I noticed the framed images leaning against the wall. I hadn't really paid attention to them because the frames were somewhat obscured by heavy vibhuti dust. The vibhuti dust had dropped from a thick collection of the substance that blanketed a large image of Sai Baba high above them. Inside the frames, nearly in the middle of the indecipherable images was a large splotch of either tumeric or cum cum. A pile of the powders accumulated in front of the photos, below the splotches, in a bin-like container. There was also a smaller photograph sitting in what appeared to be a round copper plate that was emitting vibhuti.

I saw it, and by then I believed it, but it was all so simply displayed. There was no fanfare. It simply was what it was. If Rameshji had not explained the set-up, I would not have understood what was going on.

When I saw the pile of tumeric I thought of the messages that I'd been told arrived through writing on a sheet of tumeric.

"So where do you keep the divine fax?" I asked, not knowing if I had overlooked it as well.

"Oh yes, it is there," Rameshji replied, and promptly walked to the other side of the altar.

Beneath a highly decorated Shirdi Sai Baba statue and a photo of a young, waving Sathya Sai Baba, was a wooden case with a glass top and an open front. Through the glass I could see a silver tray approximately nine by twelve inches in size, and perhaps two inches deep. Inside the tray was maybe an inch of flattened tumeric. The plain, yellowish powder totally covered the bottom of the dish, but there was no writing.

"It is easy to put in and out this way," Rameshji indicated with his hand through the opening.

"Yes, I can see it would be," I replied.

The divine fax had been given a protected place of distinction, and from a respectful distance the writing could be viewed by anyone who was interested in reading it, and it would be kept free of debris.

The last thing Rameshji brought to our attention before we walked outside was Bharosha Ma's discharge summary.

That day the weather was balmy and sunny as Rameshji explained the shrines embedded in the wall that enclosed their property. Buddha, Ganesha, Nagakal, Durga, a Shiva Lingam, a mosque, Shiva, Jesus, Krishna and Hanuman were among the beings who overlooked their lawn bordered by flowers, flowering bushes, and sprinkled with trees, mostly palms.

Rameshji became quite animated when we stopped in front of the Nagakal, an image of two vertical intertwined serpents.

"You see the small space there beneath the image?" He asked.

I squatted. I could see a square opening underneath the bas relief.

"White colored snakes live there," he continued. "We have seen them." His eyes widened with conviction. "And we have also put a small bowl of milk there for them to drink."

I'm sure my eyes widened at that point.

"A white snake is a very sacred thing," Rameshji said, "and they have lived under this shrine for many years. They are also tail-less."

I squinted. "They have no tails?"

"No. No tails. They are *nagas*. One day a pair of intertwined snakes, tail-less, were standing upward here, for a length of time. I have seen them."

We followed the walkway pass the back entrance of main bhajan hall and arrived at the Goddess Temple.

"This temple was built by one man, Ganesh Shreshta. It is the most recent of the buildings."

I examined the ornate domed edifice. "He built it by himself. Wow. He is quite the architect."

"Yes, he is," Rameshji replied. "But the first man who came to help us build a temple here was not."

"He wasn't an architect," I said.

"No. He simply showed up one day and asked if we were going to build a temple." Rameshji shook his head. "I did not know this man. But I responded to his question and told him yes we are. He told me he wanted to help. So I asked him if he had built a temple before, and said, 'No'." Rameshji's eyes brightened as if he had been told an amusing joke. "I thought how is he offering to help us build a temple if he doesn't know what to do? But I also thought, because of the way he showed up, that Baba might have sent him, so I ended up telling him to come back the next day. Well, that man began to receive dreams from Baba, and every morning he would come with instructions. Baba was directing him on a daily basis through dreams."

"Amazing," I replied. "Simply amazing."

"But as you can see this is the Goddess Temple that Ganesh has done so very nicely."

I walked through the decorative wrought iron gate and stood at the bottom of three stairs. From there I could see through a domed opening into the building, but it was secured with a protective gate. Still I noticed something I had noticed before, but with everything being so new to me it was something else to take in. I could see a brilliant orange powder around the throats of the Goddesses.

"What is that orange powder?" I asked.

Rameshji who was standing outside the iron gate replied, "What?"

"There is a beautiful orange powder like vibhuti on their necks. I can see it above their saris."

"Ohh. It is called vermillion powder. It began to manifest when we put them here and did prayer."

Of all the manifested powders I had seen this one seem to call to me the most. "It is absolutely beautiful," I replied.

"Yes," Rameshji said. "This powder only comes here in the Goddess Temple and on the silver manifest Durga in the main puja hall."

I looked back at him. "It doesn't come anywhere else?"

"No."

I stood there looking at this amazing sight of three magnificent Goddesses through whom a life force of brilliant orange Shakti could be seen. For the moment I was able to connect to all that I had been experiencing with Bharosha Ma and Rameshji. For that moment I was present. It was all very real.

"Come," Rameshji called. "Let us go. There is another bhajan hall I want to show you."

Just that quickly I was back to being an observer, although I was no longer a sincerely questioning skeptic. I was the compliant leaf.

In retrospect I understand and appreciate my basically steady frame of mind. I truly believe I would not have been able to sustain the level of intensity that I experienced outside the Goddess Temple and continue to function normally. It wouldn't have been possible.

We walked behind the temple and entered another bhajan hall that was much larger than the main one. An abundance of framed renditions of Hindu gods and goddesses, Shirdi Sai Baba, Jesus and Sathya Sai Baba hung on the walls. The entire front of the room was set against a backdrop of midnight blue sky sprinkled with stars and a full moon. Shrines of white bricks built into various shapes rose in front of it. Within each shrine, more gods and goddesses were honored, including Buddha. A white brick shelf formed the foundation. It was the lid to a rectangular enclosure beneath the shrines that spanned the entire front of the room. Inside of it, photos of deities mingled.

In the center of it all was a large shrine dedicated

to Lakshmi, Durga and Saraswati, with nearly life size images of Sathya Sai and Shirdi Sai standing guard. A garlanded photograph of Sai Baba's feet was in the center. Below it was a pair of life size padukas, silver sandals, similar to the ones the Avatar actually wears during special ceremonies.

We walked about as Rameshji talked a bit, and then we arrived in front of a yellow robe encased in glass.

"This is one of Baba's robes," he announced.

"Sai Baba gave it to you?"

Rameshji's expression changed to one that was becoming very familiar. I knew he was about to say something unusual.

"This robe manifested in Bharosha's closet." He paused for impact. "It is one of his real, silk robes. When Bharosha removed it from her closet, vibhuti ohms appeared on it. These are the kinds of things that happen here because of Bharosha. When she is not here, when we are in India or traveling…nothing happens."

I looked at the robe, believing what Rameshji had said, but once again at that safe distance.

Rameshji, who I have come to see as the ultimate observer, never hesitated in saying the manifestations did not occur without Bharosha Ma; thereby acknowledging the connection between her and Sai Baba; one that strengthened exponentially after her death. Rameshji was now a willing observer, but years before he was an observer who for a very long time, refused to see what was happening right before his eyes.

CHAPTER 28

After lunch Nancy decided to meditate in the room and I went out to do more exploring. As I descended the stairs I bumped into Bharosha Ma. She beckoned for me to follow her. Together we walked past the kitchen and exited at the end of the hall onto a balcony with two birds in large cages.

Bharosha Ma smiled as she approached a minor bird in the largest cage. She spoke to him in Nepali. Then I heard her say 'Sai Ram'. After a few repetitions the minor bird called 'Sai Ram' over and over again. Bharosha Ma turned her attention to the other bird, a parrot, before she took my hand in a gesture that indicated she wanted me to follow her again.

Next we dropped by the kitchen and Bharosha Ma introduced me to three women who were cleaning utensils and cutting up vegetables. It's amazing how well hand gestures and smiles work under a situation like that. I believe two of the women were Bhutanese and the other was from Mongolia. Later I learned that the eldest woman had served in the Adhikari household since Sujata was a child. The other, a woman perhaps in her late 20s, early 30s, had offered her help much more recently after she experienced some of the miracles.

We left the kitchen and walked outside. I watched Bharosha Ma tend a tulsi plant, a small bush that is special to many Hindu women. It was flourishing in a heavy ceramic planter on top of the wall in back of the main bhajan hall. There she spoke to another caged bird and fed it seeds.

We shared a companionable silence as she showed me a large fish pond, built in to the rear of the deck, occupied by koi and lotus plants. The air of introduction and exploration continued as we went down a stairway and emerged out on a very large plot of land, outside the property wall. I realized it was a huge garden.

I crossed the rows and rows of potatoes and cauliflower behind Bharosha Ma, navigated two tricky boards, and eventually reached a point that was almost in the center. There she turned to me with bright eyes. "Ashram," she said, moving her arm in a slow, sweeping fashion across the land.

Back then I took it for granted that they would build an ashram encompassing that entire garden space; a plot that appeared to extend from the road in front of Bharosha Ma and Rameshji's property, to the road in front of the houses behind their property. At the time I didn't consider how this would be done. I had no idea that all of the money they had received to do what they had done thus far had been accomplished through donations, donations that were not outwardly solicited. I guess I couldn't imagine that someone could build so much with or on what most would call faith. But with the Adhikaris, especially Bharosha Ma's story, I know it was built with much more than that, and the ashram will be as well.

The next day consisted of more conversations at breakfast with Rameshji and lots of shopping. When we, Bharosha Ma, Asha, Nancy, me and another devotee, emerged from Maharajgunj Chakrapath, the Adhikari's street, I witnessed the presence of the Nepalese army for the first time. Men in army uniforms and rifles got out of several vehicles as we briskly walked toward a shopping district. Bharosha Ma and the other Nepalese women didn't seem to mind, nor did the large number of people on the streets. The soldiers were simply a part of what was.

We went to two shops that sold "sawal kameez", lovely tunic and pant sets and another that sold saris. At each location with Asha's helped Bharosha Ma asked which colors and designs we preferred. More than a little astonished to be taken shopping in such a way we somewhat shyly made our preferences known. By the time saris were being chosen Nancy absolutely declined, but I knew how important it was to Bharosha Ma to show her love through giving this way as well, so I chose a couple of beautiful saris, but I definitely felt humbled by her bounteous generosity.

Throughout the remainder of the day I heard various miraculous accounts that had occurred at the Adhikari's home through the years. How Bharosha Ma was cooking and realized she didn't have any kerosene, but Sai Baba allowed the stove to burn as if there was a full supply. There was an account of a large candy ball that simply appeared above Rameshji's head, and a day when their grandson Prashant, who was brought home a photo of Baba that still hangs in the kitchen to this day. Prashant said Baba had given it to him.

Over the next couple of days Nancy turned 66 and I sat in on many conversations with Bharosha Ma , Madhavi, Asha and Jyoti. By then it how become clear to me that Madhavi and Asha assisted Bharosha Ma almost everyday in the bhajan halls and the temple. Both women spoke English very well and served as interpreters, which I really appreciated. I also met Bharosha Ma's, sister, Bunu, and came to feel quite close to Prajwol's wife, Apurna.

Rameshji led an outing the next day to his mother's house which, by taxi, was a short distance away from the Adhikari's home. We had to get out and walk the remainder of the way when the cab driver refused to drive down a deeply rutted road. It was the main access road to the road in front of her house, a nice two storied white structure surrounded by a small fence.

Rameshji's very petite mother, Sita, and several of Rameshji's relatives welcomed us with tea, food and coca-cola. We socialized in the living room where a large portrait of Rameshji's father, Tejraj Adhikari, hung prominently on a wall. Later Sitadevi offered to show us her shrine nestled in an alcove not far from her bedroom. We said a prayer and a light spray of vibhuti came on the collection of Hindu deities. Afterwards Prajwol and Bunti, Ramesji's nephew, took Nancy and me to an amazing Tibetan monastery that could be seen in the distance from the back of the property.

After we returned, when we were in our room, Nancy admitted she found the difference between East and West broader than she had imagined. We discussed the cultural differences which we were experiencing as the Adhikari's guests in predominately Hindu Nepal. One thing was true, basically we were not encouraged to go out alone. I felt, because of the trouble the Nepalese government was having with the Maoists, the Adhikaris were rightfully concerned about our safety; the care we were being given was an honor. Nancy found the protective environment more challenging, and expressed reservations about having made the journey.

The next day Siru and Lily, Bharosha Ma and Rameshji's daughters, along with Siru's boys, Prashant and Siraj, came to take us shopping. This time Nancy declined, but Apurna and I joined them in a day of acquiring an array of tikas, beautiful self-adhesive jewelry for the third eye, and the acquisition of a lovely jade and coral necklace for me. We ate pizza at a small restaurant and I sampled some of the hot and sweet snacks Apurna learned to love from childhood. They proved to be much too hot for me.

Nancy was a little rattled by the time I returned. Despite her toe that still pained her, Nancy said she attempted to take a walk by herself, but when she was a short distance down the street one of women who helped around the house chased her down and insisted that she return. As each day passed she seemed to find the Adhikari's protective attitude more and more confining.

CHAPTER 29

The following morning before bhajans Bharosha Ma came for me. We met Madhavi in front of the Goddess Temple where she promptly produced a key, and unlocked the interior wrought iron door that protected the precious deities. I recall how I felt that to be the keeper of the key of the goddesses was such an honor for Madhavi.

Once we were inside Bharosha Ma spoke to Madhavi. Promptly Madhavi went over to Saraswati and removed a yellow beaded necklace from her throat. Bharosha Ma turned to me and said, “Gold.”

I looked at the necklace. An inch long golden cylinder hung in the middle of multiple strands of yellow beads.

Bharosha Ma took the necklace from Madhavi’s hands and fastened it around my throat. I was astounded by this gift. Simply astounded. I looked at Madhavi and I looked at Bharosha Ma. There was a satisfied, determined look on Bharosha Ma’s face. I didn’t know what to make of what she had done, and I was so full. All I could do was cry.

Bharosha Ma followed that by removing a strand of small beaded necklaces from all three of the goddesses. She gave those to me as well before we left the temple and I returned to my room.

More sightseeing and shopping followed the next

day. Bharosha Ma took us, her two grandsons and a female devotee who spoke English, to the world famous Kathesimbhu Stupa. This time, no matter how she tried, Nancy could not turn down the saris, bangles and earrings that were purchased.

We left the busy area and headed to Lily's house, a spacious, elegant home where we were served tea and soft drinks. Lily spoke of how she had asked Baba for a large home (Lily's home was a miniature palace) and how she had asked for a child. She said Sai Baba told her to come to Puttaparthi and he would give her a child. Her daughter Shivani was conceived and born a short time afterwards.

We rested after we returned to the Adhikari's, and then Nancy and I wandered into the main bhajan hall where we saw Rameshji removing the divine fax, the tray of tumeric, from its protected space.

"You have been out shopping again with Bharosha," he said.

I think we laughed a little and replied affirmatively.

"She enjoys giving you things."

"It's very obvious and very appreciated," I said before I asked. "So what are you doing, Rameshji?"

"No messages have come from Baba since our return from America," he replied. "They have not come because we have not asked Swami."

Carefully, he placed the divine fax on the floor before he sat down beside it. Next Rameshji picked up a photo of Shirdi Sai Baba and began to systematically press it down on the tumeric.

"I am preparing the tumeric for a message," he said as he leveled the yellow powder. "There has been no message so we must ask him."

Once his task was complete, Rameshji got up and

returned the tray to its place under the glass. He picked up the photo of Shirdi Sai Baba, looked at Nancy and me and said, "Now we will see what Baba does."

There was excitement in the air when a message arrived the next day. From a purely observation point of view, the letters were very even and the rows uncannily straight. Although I could not read it, I thought it would be virtually impossible for a human being to write in the soft powder without a slippage of any sort. There didn't appear to be a place where a word or even a letter cut too deep, or caused some of the tumeric to form the slightest unsightly pile. The writing and the depth of each letter appeared to be exactly the same, appeared to be perfect. It said:

> You do 11 bhajans. Ramesh, Bharosha, you did a very good job. You did very well in America. Swami is happy. Do love all. Swami has given blessings to all American devotees. Take the guests to Nagarkot for sightseeing place. All devotees, everyone, love the guests. They deserve your love. You have to love. Ramesh, Bharosha take the guests many places. Swami always gives opportunity to work and you always obey whatever I say. Swami loves you.

So after the message we prepared to go to Nagarkot. For the occasion, Bharosha Ma, Madhavi and Apurna dressed us in saris, and a small van was quickly secured. In a couple of hours, twelve of us were on our way to the site.

We sang bhajans on the way, and Prashant who was 10 years old kept singing 'Say The Name of Sathya Sai', a bhajan with a catchy tune he picked up from me. There were snacks galore. It was a very lighthearted excursion.

As we drew nearer to Nagacourt, the scene beside the upward spiraling road was breathtaking. Utterly massive hills were tiered and curved to perfection. But by the time we arrived at the lookout point, the clouds had descended and Mount Everest and the Himalayas were mere fathoms.

But that didn't stop us from picnicking in a nearby area where I embarrassed myself to the hilt. I ingested a handful of a snack that several of the women were enjoying. Immediately after I swallowed a bit of it, I knew I was in trouble. For me it was excruciatingly spicy. I gagged and coughed as if my life depended on it, while the group looked surprised then concerned, and once I had nearly recovered, there were a few suppressed smiles.

CHAPTER 30

Every morning Bharosha Ma and Rameshji took a walk, and on this particular morning I was invited to join them. We started out around 7 a.m. when the neighborhoods had just begun to stir. A waking quiet embraced us as we advanced up Maharajgunj Chakrapath, passing gated homes, school girls in uniforms, and a few people walking in silent contemplation. Only one or two cars passed us on that road, and there was a minor increase in traffic when we entered a tiny business district.

Vendors were opening stall-like stores stocked with vegetables and/or sundry goods. There was a vegetable man with an ample amount of product on the back of his bicycle riding by, and another man delivering vegetables at one of the stalls. As we continued on our way we saw a vendor with live chickens in cages and there was a man who had just slaughtered a lamb. The head of the lifeless animal lay as a tribute to its sacrifice on the side of the road.

At first we walked in silence and that was fine by me. There was so much to observe, but as we progressed Rameshji began to talk about some of the tribulations they experienced because of Bharosha Ma and the manifestations.

"Baba has written, and he has also said, that we should protect Bharosha Ma," he began. "This is very important," Rameshji said, as he walked and looked at the ground. "When the statues and other objects first started coming, and more and more people began to know about them, there were people who were not pleased. They wondered and asked why are these things only coming at Ramesh Nepali's house. Why don't they come at some other Sai devotees' homes? Some who have been devotees of Swami much longer than he has."

"But Mommie has been a Sai Baba devotee all of her life," I said.

"Of course," Rameshji replied. "But there was talk like this. There was all kinds of talk. Negative things, and there were threats of poisoning."

"Someone threatened to kill you?"

"Yes." He nodded slowly.

"And this was before Bharosha Mommie died?

"Yes," he said again. "You see vibhuti has been coming for years. But then there was an acceleration in the manifestations after I lost my job in 1992. Bharosha died in Puttaparthi in 1995."

I had not considered the possibility of people reacting to the phenomenon surrounding Bharosha Ma in such way. "It's horrible that you would have to deal with something like that."

"Ye-es, but we did," Rameshji said slowly. "Another time we came home and someone had set fire to our house."

"They tried to burn down your house?" I was truly shocked.

"Yes. Part of the house did burn. I remember going inside the building where there was lots of smoke and saying to Baba that we were his devotees and he was supposed to protect us. When I said that blood began to flow from the lingam."

"Wait a minute. Blood was coming—"

"Blood was coming out of the top of the lingam. The one that manifested in the puja room."

"How do you know that it was blood?"

"I know blood when I see it. Wouldn't you?"

I thought about it for a second. "I would."

"You would," Rameshji said with conviction. "It came from the lingam and began to bubble as if it were boiling. That bubbling blood flowed into the plate below the lingam, and I knew it was a special way that Baba chose to answer me." He looked at me as he spoke. "And I said 'Don't worry. I have the house. It has burned but I have my son and my house. So don't worry.' And the blood stopped. Almost a half a liter of blood came that day."

I looked at Bharosha Ma but she didn't look my way. She just continued to walk, in silence, on the other side of Rameshji.

"We got through that," Rameshji continued, "and someone knocked down the front portion of the wall that surrounds our house."

"No-o."

"They did. They knocked the wall down and we had to rebuild it as well. But after they did that, there was a united front from some of the Sai devotees. These devotees responded to what had happened to us. They linked hands and formed a human chain around our property."

"Showing that they stood with you and Bharosha Ma."

"Yes."

"Oh my goodness. So, is there a Sai Baba community Center here in Kathmandu?"

"Yes. I will show it to you one day we are on an outing. It is not far from our home."

I thought about that. "But some of those devotees don't believe the manifestations that are happening around Bharosha Ma are real."

"That is correct," Rameshji answered. "So this is what has happened, and Baba has said we must protect Bharosha. Swami has said to protect Bharosha is to protect Mother Earth."

"Really. Why does he say that?"

"Swami says Bharosha is Mother Earth."

I became quiet. I felt very concerned for Bharosha Ma, Rameshji and their family. I had been shown so much loving kindness, I simply wanted to be able to do something to give back.

"What can I do to help, Rameshji?" I asked.

"The book about Bharosha that you have been inspired to write; I see it as a continuation of your previous work, because you have consistently written about the oneness of humanity. That is Swami's teaching. If Baba allows you to write the book and to get it out to the public, you will be of help."

By that time we arrived at our first temple. It was a very small structure dedicated to Durga. To me, the energy around it felt as if the building had been there a very long time; that the prayers and supplications were deeply rooted. We stopped at the temple and said a silent prayer.

I prayed with my fresh concern about their safety in my heart. I prayed about what I had seen and witnessed since meeting Bharosha Ma, and for my ability to tell the story if it was God's will. When I was done I was surprised when a significant bolt of external energy entered my heart.

I opened my eyes and Rameshji was encouraging me to follow Bharosha Ma. The three of us circled the small stone edifice with the Goddess powerfully tucked inside, as a decorative bas relief of amorous Gods and Goddesses frolicked near the top of the building. Once the circle was complete Bharosha Ma rang a bell that hung from a corner of the roof. I rang it too and we continued on.

CHAPTER 31

The entire walk took about an hour. As we drew near to the house Bharosha Ma purchased several vegetables from a couple of the storekeepers. They would be included in our meal that day.

While Nancy and I sat in our room, Madhavi, Apurna and Jyoti stopped in. They told me how lucky I was to receive the gold necklace that had hung around Saraswati's neck. Madhavi was the most adamant. She emphasized the power of the prayers that had been infused into the ornament.

Soon after, Bharosha Ma, Siru and Rameshji came to the door. Perhaps there had been more talk about the necklace I received because Siru posed a question about an earlier gift from Bharosha Ma.

"Did you know Baba gave Mommie the red bangles she gave to you?"

Stunned I looked at Mommie. "No."

"He did," Siru said, standing close behind her mother.

Mommie simply nodded like a shy girl, before she said something to Rameshji.

"Bharosha says when she first saw you she felt that you were her daughter."

Mommie smiled, looked at me and nodded.

"I think that is why there's such a big attraction between you," Rameshji added. "Bharosha and you are like pure gold and diluted gold. There is something pure in Bharosha and something pure in you. Therefore this attraction, and a kind of melding is occurring."

When they left the room, Nancy said she felt as if I was being adorned like one of the goddesses, and that she believed I had a special role to play in Bharosha Ma's life. She explained to me that the transmission that she was scheduled to receive from Genpo Roshi was also a kind of melding.

Another message arrived from Sai Baba the following day. Several things were mentioned. Rameshji also told us that Baba said he was paying special attention to us, Nancy and me, the guests.

That afternoon Bharosha Ma, Lily, Siru, Madhavi, Asha, Nancy and me went to Lily's boutique in an upscale part of town, where Lily and her husband sold high end Pashmina shawls, products of her husband's factory. I purchased one for myself and one for Jan, with money she had provided for that purpose.

Afterwards some of us continued on to Swayambhunath, the Monkey Temple, where we were warned not to make eye contact with the baboons. They might run off with our purses or do something else unexpected.

We peered inside the temple, like the one that could be seen in the distance from Rameshji's mother's home, it was absolutely beautiful. But unlike that temple Swayambhunath was surrounded by merchants selling items such as jewelry, clothing, home decorations and tankards. I bought a Nepalese coat for Larry and myself, some incense to donate to the puja room, and a small tin container with Sai Baba's photograph on it. When I returned to the Adhikaris, I placed it on the altar and hoped

I'd receive something from Baba.

After bhajans that evening a man carrying a brick came into the main bhajan hall. He gave it to Rameshji and they spoke for a brief while. Rameshji placed the brick at the base of the shrine near the divine fax as the man left. I approached Rameshji and asked him why the brick had become a part of the shrine.

"Whatever we do we offer it to Baba first so that He will bless us with success. We will start building a third floor very soon. Baba has said on more than one occasion that many people will come. He said in the last message that many Americans will come, so we are doing what we can at this time to prepare."

I understood Rameshji offered the brick because it represented another phase of construction, another part of the overall plan for an ashram. The Adhikaris were preparing for the devotees who Sai Baba promised would come.

"There have been visitors through the years," Rameshji continued. "They have come from several countries, but Baba says many Americans will come. If they come now where will we put them? We must be prepared for the devotees."

CHAPTER 32

After morning tea and breakfast, somewhat disappointed, Nancy and I returned to our room. A trip to Taulihawa, Kapilbastu in Lumbini had been cancelled. After listening to news reports, we were forced to accept a mudslide had blocked the main road to the town and we would not be able to get through. We would not be able to visit the area where Bharosha Ma and the Buddha were born.

I was updating my journal when Rameshji appeared in our open doorway. Throughout the house an open door was a kind of standing, silent invitation, therefore it was quite common for visitors to wander in. Bharosha Ma and Rameshji acknowledged as the number of devotees who visited their property increased the rules would have to change, but at the time of our visit we had been wholly embraced as the Adhikari's personal guests.

"I would like to show you these today," Rameshji said as he walked into the room, carrying a small jewelry case in his hand. "Baba manifested them over a period of two months. There are eight diamonds here as you will see. He also manifested a diamond ring made of gold."

Rameshji opened the case, and I got up from where I was sitting on my bed for a closer to look. There were eight diamonds, just as he said, each progressively larger than the other.

"The stones were smaller in the beginning," he continued, "but they have been growing...."

"Growing?" I found I often repeated what was said to me when confronting concepts outside of common logic. Although I vaguely remember Rameshji mentioning the growing diamonds when we were in Salt Lake, it was quite different standing there, looking at the actual stones and processing the notion that they could grow.

"Yes," he emphatically stated. "That is what is happening. They are growing."

"How long ago did they manifest?" My logical mind was having a tough time with this one.

"About two years ago. They came over a two-month period."

I looked at the sparkly collection of round princess cut diamonds. Even to my untrained, limited experience eyes I could tell they were of the highest quality. There was an amazing clarity and color to the stones. All of them appeared to be flawless which most jewelers would probably say is impossible, but I guess if the Avatar could manifest a diamond it would be no less than absolutely perfect.

"I wonder why Baba manifested eight.' The first thing that came into my head came out of my mouth.

"I feel it has something to do with the planets," Rameshji replied. "From the smallest planet to the largest one, the diamonds are a reflection of that. I think so,' he said, but there was uncertainty in his voice.

Later I asked Rameshji if I could take a photograph of the unusual stones. He obliged me by bringing out the case and holding up the largest diamond, and maybe one or two of the others. I still have one of the photographs but because I'm not a professional photographer, once again, like the photo of my favorite banana it is out of focus. The other photographs were totally hopeless.

Part of the day was spent visiting another Nepalese home where we were treated with food and gifts. At that home, like all the others, vibhuti appeared on sacred images. I can't recall who told me, but I came to understand that the visits Bharosha Ma was making to devotee's homes in Kathmandu was something new. That after the threats and actions taken against them, outside of family, Bharosha Ma and Rameshji stayed close to home. It appeared our coming to Kathmandu had initiated a new phase of interaction between Bharosha Ma and the devotees.

That evening several female devotees, including Madhavi gifted me with three beautiful saris. One of women, Sarada Auntie, sister of the deceased King Birendra, gave me what is called a principle sari. It was an amazingly thin, in my estimation lemon yellow. Sarada Auntie said she was going to start calling me Gauri, another name for Shiva's wife.

In light of all the generosity, Nancy told me I was being dressed up and empowered like one of the Goddesses and that there was something anthropological about it. Nancy said she wondered where it would end. It was also obvious that her discomfort with our confinement, as she saw it, had increased. She believed there would come a time when we would not be allowed to leave. I didn't know why, but that's how she saw it, and she felt a contingency plan was necessary. I tried to discuss it with her, to gain some understanding but her fear was real, and the foundation of a difficult situation was well under way.

During our short acquaintance I had come to respect Nancy, and up until the time of what was unfolding I considered her to be a logical person, so I tried to consider the things that she was saying, but they simply didn't work for me. I could only see the love and sincerity that was being showered upon us, and I told her so.

The following morning construction began on a brand new third floor. Bright and early we could hear the construction crew talking through our open windows. We could also hear the forceful sounds of the roof being removed, so I decided to visit with Rameshji and Bharosha Ma in their room. I had perfect timing because Sujata happen to call. She was excited. She believed another operation had been performed on her throat. Sujata asked if a message had come from Baba about it. As quick as a whip Bharosha Ma informed her no message had come, and there would be no message that day.

With everything that was unfolding, it still struck me with wonder at how clear Bharosha Ma's communications were with Sai Baba.

There was also talk of a dream. Bharosha Ma had dreamed about her grandparents. In the dream they were putting cum cum on their foreheads, and they were telling Bharosha Ma that she should buy a particular plot of land. I could tell this was important information, and although Rameshji was interpreting for me, because I didn't know the background of the situation I didn't know what land was being discussed. In short order the state of affairs became clear. The day before Bharosha Ma had the dream Rameshji received a phone call from his sick brother offering to sell a certain piece of property.

Tiffin, a meal between lunch and dinner, was scheduled that day at the home of Mahae and Sasat Kiran. They had been Sai Baba devotees for 30 years. Sasat Kiran was the founder of the Sathya Sai Baba organization in Nepal and she had also worked as a Secretary of Education for the country.

I could tell there was something significant about this particular visit so I dressed in one of my prettiest saris. Whenever we were alone, and only when we were alone did Nancy speak of how uneasy she was feeling. The locks on the windows and the door of our bedroom deeply concerned her, although the same windows and doors were used throughout the Adhikari house and in some of the Nepalese homes that we had visited.

She felt particular antsy that day. We had been informed that we would have to wait a couple of days before our next bank visit. Nancy thought that was a very bad omen and that our situation was becoming quite dire.

I write of what was happening between us not to demean Nancy in any way, but because what happened between us is important to this memoir. I struggled with if what happened with Nancy should be included, but not to include how our relationship in Kathmandu unfolded would leave a gapping hole in an important upcoming event.

Nancy's perception of our situation and my opposition to it created a kind of pressure cooker whenever we were behind the closed door of our bedroom. The scheduled but delayed trip to the bank, and the fact that I had not spoken to Larry in several days was proof, according to Nancy that things were going very awry. I was concerned that I had not spoken to Larry, but I was concerned that something may have happened to him in America, not that his calls were being kept from me.

There is a saying that Sai Baba is famous for, "Help ever. Hurt never." I leaned very heavily on that principle over the next few days. I told Nancy, if what she believed was true, and we were not allowed to go to the bank on the day that we were scheduled to go, that I would begin to consider what she was saying. It was the only way that I could buy time to allow the truth, as I saw it, to unfold. You may ask why didn't I tell the Adhikaris what was going on. I didn't know how to tell these people who were doing so much, that they're loving actions were being perceived as a threat. Nor did I want to hurt Nancy.

The Kiran's home was quite stately. The furnishings and decorations reminded me of well established homes in America where the owners were people of means. It was the first home that we visited where our meal was actually served by a servant, a young Nepalese boy.

After we consumed our meal and tea had been served, we exited the main portion of the house and entered into a courtyard. On the opposite side of the landscaped area was another brick building. With the Kiran's leading the way, we mounted stairs to that building and entered a large puja room, a very comfortable space with a beautifully lit photograph of Sai Baba mounted on the front wall. There was also a painting of Sai Baba's feet.

Once we were situated on the floor in front of the photo there was a moment of indecisive quiet. I could feel something was at stake but I didn't know what. That's when Rameshji took the reins, and at his behest Bharosha Ma, Asha, Madhavi, Jyoti and I began to sing bhajans, maybe three before we stopped. An uncertain silence rose again before Rameshji announced that we should all leave the bhajan hall and let Swami do his work.

That's what we did. We descended the stairs and reentered the Kiran's home. We had been sitting in what

I would call a parlor for perhaps a minute or two, when Bharosha Ma indicated that she could smell a sacred fragrance. With her declaration, we returned to the puja room where a substantial spray of vibhuti had manifested on the large photograph of Sai Baba. A smaller manifestation of the ash was on the painting of his feet, and that's when I got it. The manifested vibhuti in the Kiran's puja room absolutely proved to them that the manifestations and the spiritual accounts surrounding Bharosha Ma were valid.

After we witnessed the miracle, to close the ceremony, the Kiran's gave us some of their vibhuti. I ingested some which was customary, and found the taste quite different from the vibhuti I had tasted before. Later I shared my observation with Rameshji and he informed me that most likely the ash had been purchased in India; that this was quite common, and although the vibhuti was considered to be blessed by Sai Baba it had not been manifested by Sai Baba. I realized because of my association with the Rimals and Adhikaris, it was my first taste of vibhuti that had not actually been manifested by the Avatar. That evening when a core group of devotees gathered for tea after bhajans, something that was a repeated recent occurrence, I felt as if an account was being giving about our visit to the Kiran's home.

I had come to cherish the orderly social gathering in the back of the Adhikaris main bhajan hall. Basically, we sat in a circle and enjoyed a final serving of hot tea. Small metal cups of chai with sugar cubes would be offered and quickly consumed by everyone except for me. My capabilities required a somewhat cooler brew. But when the temperature was right I enjoyed it as well. That particular night I also enjoyed the gentle conversations, the soft laughter and the proof that manifested in the Kiran's puja room.

CHAPTER 33

After a bit of enquiry I found out that Mayatri, the woman who asked if she could work at the Adhikaris after witnessing some of the miracles, cleaned and prepared the altar in the main bhajan hall every morning. I thought this was such an honorable job that I wanted to watch her ministrations, and I also wanted to see the flower jump on top of the manifested lingam.

So I rose early the next morning and joined the working women in the kitchen. We had become quite comfortable with each other. Through sign language, pointing and many smiles we had established a basic level of communication, and I was able to tell Mayatri that I wanted to join her during her morning task. With a modest smile, she invited me and my camera, to follow her down to the puja room.

I sat and watched her reposition photographs and brass vases, refill candle-like lamps with mustard seed oil, and make sure an adequate amount of home-made cotton wick was available for lighting. I took a few pictures while Mayatri cleaned up the ashes left over from burnt incense and any other debris that cluttered the front of the altar.

Once that was done, she signaled for me to follow her outside while she gathered fresh blossoms from blooming plants, among them were hibiscus and jasmine.

We reentered the puja room where Mayatri placed the blossoms within the base of the manifested Shiva lingam. I took another photograph, and from that moment, for me, the watch was on. I stared at the small, ornate item wondering when... if... a flower would actually jump on top of the protruding stone. While I was waiting for the miracle, Mayatri was gathering up her tools and the debris. The next thing I knew she was beckoning for me to follow her once again. I was hesitant, and she could tell. But Mayatri's gesture conveyed the same message that Rameshji had said at the Kiran's home, "Let us leave so Swami can do his work".

Reluctantly, I followed her through the back door of the bhajan hall. Mayatri threw the debris which consisted of dried flower petals and ashes into a flower bed before she knelt down in front of some copper vases and began to wash them. I took a maybe two more photographs but then I was at a loss. So I walked around to the front door of the Adhikari's home, stood there a moment before I retraced my steps and reentered the bhajan hall. To my amazement and surprise, a small, extremely delicate jasmine blossom was precariously perched on top of the Shiva lingam, while the other blossoms looked as if they had been puffed up by a magical burst of air. Satisfied but somewhat dismayed that I had not actually seen the flower jump, I took another photograph and returned to my room.

That day Bharosha Ma announced that she would prepare and cook *ma-mos*. Sanjay was the first person I ever heard speak of the vegetable dumplings. More than once back in Salt Lake City I heard him ask his mother, Sujata, to repeat how he had eaten a dozen or more of the tasty dish during a visit to Nepal. The ma-mos seem to naturally create an air of how many can you eat, and even generate competition. Prashant and Siraj, Siru's sons, predicted between the two of them who would eat the most.

About mid-morning, very large pots of boiling water steamed on top of the stove as Bharosha Ma and some of the women who helped around the property sat on the floor cutting up vegetables into tiny pieces,. With practiced fingers small amounts of the vegetables were placed on a flat, circular piece of dough. They folded the vegetables inside and then sealed the edges. As soon as there was a respectable batch, the ma-mos were tossed into the boiling water, as more ma-mos were being prepared.

I tried my hand at making a few, and when I placed them with the others it was quite obvious which ones were mine. Now this was not a formal sit down everyone take a plate deal. Whenever the fresh, hot dumplings were removed from the boiling water whoever was available and ready, ate them. I must admit with Bharosha Ma's encouragement, I ate the delicious ma-mos until I felt I might burst.

With five meals a day, I was doing more than my fair share of eating in Kathmandu, and my rapidly tightening clothes were proof of it. Although after several pleas for mercy, Nancy and I managed to cut our meals down to a mere three. But it seemed to me Bharosha Ma was happiest with these simple pleasures, feeding and clothing others, making sure no one went without, happy to be able to make others happy.

That day, a childhood friend of Bharosha Ma's, Sapkota, showed up at the Adhikari's house. She was a diminutive woman with a face that reflected the countryside. I learned that Sapkota worked at a comptroller's office, and while we sat in the main bhajan hall with the sun shining in, she spoke of their childhood together.

"We were bosom friends," Sapkota said. "Bharosha always showed a deep love for her friends. She always fed others if she ate, and she never kept anything for herself. Bharosha started being a Sai Baba devotee when she was a child and I remember how vibhuti came in her home throughout our childhood. Vibhuti, amrit and ohms would come on the side of water glasses."

Eventually Sapkota began to talk about how she had gone to Puttaparthi to see Sai Baba, and how for six days she was not able to see him. Sapkota said on the seventh day she began to weep and say, "I am Bharosha's friend, why are you discriminating against me?" That day Sapkota said she was able to see the Avatar.

It was not a long visit. Soon Sapkota announced that she had to leave. Rameshji and I remained in the room as Bharosha Ma walked her outside.

"I could tell Mommie was sincerely happy to see her."

"Yes," Rameshji replied. "I think she was. And as you can tell from some of the things Sapkota said Bharosha's life was unusual even when she was a child."

"Most definitely," I replied.

"And the things you heard from Sapkota were very interesting but there were others. Bharosha has told me that she had *darshan* of Lord Krishna when she was around twelve years old."

"Darshan meaning that he appeared to her."

Rameshji nodded. "That is correct." He looked down. "And there was another interesting occurrence when she was about nine years old."

"What happened?"

"Bharosha told me she came out from her house, and her house is located where Buddha's palace is there."

"Yes."

"Bharosha came out.... And you know a tornado?"

"Ye-es?"

"It was like a tornado. It came down in a field in front of her and touched the ground, and that wind took dirt from the ground into the air."

"Okay." I visualized what he was telling me.

"Now that dirt was gone and there was a big hole left. That hole was about 12 feet in diameter. Bharosha went into the hole."

"Was she by herself?"

"She entered the hole alone," Rameshji replied. "In that hole she found a statue of Vishnu that was about two and half feet tall. So Bharosha took the statue with her. They estimated the value of that statue to be about five thousand rupees."

"Oh my. Did her family keep it?"

"No, they did not." Rameshji raised his finger. "And there is physical proof of what happened to Bharosha that day. That statue is still.... There is a building in Kapilbastu that is a children's house. Bal Mandir. That Vishnu statue is still on the second floor of that place."

Bhajans were held as usual that evening. When they were over and Nancy and I were alone in our bedroom, for the first time she spoke of making an early return to the United States.

CHAPTER 34

The next morning after Nancy insisted on going, we joined Bharosha Ma and Rameshji on their morning walk. On the way we passed the same Durga temple and Bharosha Ma did her prayer. I prayed as well. Perhaps thirty minutes later we came upon a Kali temple. Although small, it was somewhat larger than the Durga temple, yet the energy was just as old. From what I can recall, several worshippers offered incense there, adding to the thick smoke inside the structure. I saw Bharosha Ma acknowledge the Goddess with folded hands and a nod before she continued on.

Because of the smoke and the dark interior, I could barely see the goddess as she sat in her shrine, but I noticed splatters of a red liquid near the outside of the building.

"Is that blood?" I asked Rameshji.

"Yes, it is blood. But animal sacrifice is strongly discouraged in Nepal."

As we continued on our way I considered how old the Goddess temples appeared to be, and as I've stated before how old the energy felt, and I surmised some worshippers continued the rite of animal sacrifice because it had been performed by their family for generations. They would not easily let go of that way of life.

By the time we returned to the house and to our

room it was two hours later, and Nancy was hobbling. Bharosha Ma happened to stop in to retrieve something from the closet and I can't recall if it was Nancy or I who told her about Nancy's painful toe. Bharosha Ma looked at it, and with one swift motion reached out and clasped her toe. Her hand was like a fist holding Nancy's toe between her thumb and forefinger. She held it...and let go; then Bharosha Ma picked up the object she came for and left the room. Although Nancy didn't say a word I could see the sheen of tears in her eyes.

No more than an hour later word reached us that Sai Baba had delivered another message on the divine fax.

> You do 11 bhajan. You celebrate Rama Navami nicely. Feed all the people. This thing you should do altogether. Swami will help you. All devotees may/can have faith in Baba. Love Bharosha. She has come from America after doing great work. She loves all the devotees. She does because of love. Once again, I have made operation on Sujata. Now it is all right. Ramesh many people are coming from the United States/America and you have to love all. If you do Swami will be happy.

As I assumed was his ritual, Rameshji copied the message in a notebook and wrote it on a board that was posted for all to see.

Lunch was scheduled at another home. In a procession of women led by Bharosha Ma, we took a back street and cut across a field on our way to the devotee's house as a lone brahma cow grazed nearby.

The female devotee welcomed us enthusiastically before offering tea and a variety of foods including a traditional Nepalese dish of pickled potatoes. There was no need for prayers or bhajans at her home, vibhuti instantly manifested on four photographs and a statue.

The remainder of the afternoon was pleasant. Nancy and I concluded, for her, what was occurring with Bharosha Ma was an exercise of totally squashing the ego. She acknowledged her hosts and the Nepalese people were giving everything they had to welcome us, and to love us.

Before evening bhajans began I sat on the floor in the main bhajan hall with a female devotee named Lakshmi Sherestha. She was a kind woman who may have been in her 40's with a serene quality about her. After some small talk; Lakshmi spoke excellent English, she shared what had been a transforming experience. Lakshmi pointed toward a painting encased in a very ornate, dark wooden frame. It hung to the left of us. It was a young Krishna playing a flute with an adoring cow beside him.

"I was sitting in this room," she began, "with a friend of mine. We were sitting very similarly to where we are sitting now. My friend was a very strong believer in Sai Baba. I had heard many things about him, but I wasn't certain if the things I heard were true." She paused. "I thought some things may have been true, but there were so many things being said and some were quite outlandish. I didn't know what to believe. I had also heard about people Bharosha had healed, so I would come to bhajans with my friend from time to time.

That day we were sitting here, and my friend started asking Sai Baba for a flower. And I mean she was sincerely asking for this flower. I thought, how can Sai Baba give her a flower when he's in Puttaparthi? The next thing I knew a flower came out of that painting," Lakshmi pointed at the Krishna painting, "and landed in my friend's lap. I was so shocked. But then another flower came out and landed between us, and a third flower came out, and it landed in front of us. I have wholeheartedly believed in Sai Baba since then, and the manifestations that have happened here."

When Nancy and I retired to the room that night we weren't feeling well. She had developed a fever and her digestive system was in high rebellion, while my symptoms were much milder. Once again Nancy spoke of leaving early but the conversation was cut short by waves of nausea.

As usual, when morning dawned Gita delivered our tea as we still lie in bed. During the night Nancy's illness seemed to have run its course, but she told me that wasn't the only thing that she had experienced. Nancy pointed at the picture of Sai Baba that hung on our wall and said, "He came throughout the night with a warning. He told me, 'They want to hurt you.'"

"They want to hurt us?" I looked at the photograph.

"No, they don't want to hurt you. They want to hurt me."

It was an extremely uncomfortable way to start the day but I thought things were looking up when as agreed, and with Prajwol as our escort, Nancy and I went to the Himalayan Bank. We were also scheduled to attend lunch at the home of a former airline pilot with Rameshji and Bharosha Ma. Arrangements for Prajwol to return home after our banking business had been made, and Nancy and I were to proceed to the pilot's home where the Adhikaris would be waiting.

After Prajwol got out of the cab Nancy, a British citizen, insisted that she had business that needed to be taken care of at the embassy before she could return to the states. Trust had been such a factor that I wanted to uphold an air of cooperation, and we had ample time before lunch. So, we went to the British Embassy but they directed us to the American Embassy because of Nancy's green card status.

Nature called and I left Nancy to attend to my needs. When I returned I saw Nancy crying and speaking to one of the guards. At first she didn't see me, and when I entered hearing range Nancy was in an emotional disclosure of what she felt was going on at the Adhikari's home, a kidnapping of sorts.

A surprised Nancy looked into my stunned face and quickly wiped her eyes, but it was too late. I had seen and heard and couldn't believe it. All I could think about were agents being sent from the American Embassy over to the Adhikari's house and accusing them of some crime. I just couldn't believe it and there was an instant anger.

I was angry. I was appalled. But I could also see this vulnerability on her face and in her eyes. So by the time we walked outside of the embassy I told Nancy, if she truly believed what she was telling that guard, if she was truly afraid, she should go home, and that I would help her. Help ever. Hurt never.

Although I knew I would be late for lunch and that the Adhikari's were waiting, we went to the travel agency and changed Nancy's ticket. Nancy was booked on a flight to America the next day, but the ticket wouldn't be ready for pick up until later that afternoon.

I had lost my travel mate to India, and I had used self control I didn't know I possessed. I wanted to shout "How could you?!" but I didn't believe it was Nancy's intent to hurt the Adhikaris. Simply put, Nancy's reality in Kathmandu was one thing and mine was another.

It was a difficult lunch to say the least. There I was without Nancy, nearly an emotional wreck myself, but because we were the guests at another Nepalese home I could not tell Rameshji or Bharosha Ma what had happened. So under puzzled looks, I made my apologies and lunch proceeded.

Anti-American sentiment was high amongst some people because of the war. They saw us as Goliath beating up on David, a bluffing but weaponless David at that, and the pilot, my host, wanted to talk about the war and his negative view of America. He wanted to talk about it with an American, me. I was in no shape to do that nor was I in the mood. In the end, I was able to retain an air of respect for myself, for my host and for the Adhikaris. But by the time we reached the Adhikari's home and I told Rameshji about Nancy's new travel plans I was in tears.

Everyone wanted to know why Nancy wanted to leave and I attempted to explain, but it wasn't easy. There's no way I could have told them the collection of threads that had woven the tapestry that led up to that point.

For a moment Bharosha Ma tried to convince Nancy to stay, but Rameshji supported Nancy's decision to leave without really understanding why. So late that afternoon, Prajwol made a second trip to the bank and to the travel agency with Nancy and me to pick up Nancy's ticket.

I can't recall if Nancy attended bhajans that evening. I do know Madhavi and I did and we couldn't hold back the tears when Madhavi sang, 'Tera Nam Ek Sahara'. I guess Madhavi cried because Nancy was leaving. I had seen a kind of affinity develop between them. I cried because of the melancholy in Madhavi's voice, because

Nancy was leaving, and because of the differences that existed between human beings even under the best of circumstances, and the best of intentions.

As we prepared for bed the packing commenced for Nancy's return. She agreed to take several items back to Sujata and Tina, and Bharosha Ma helped to arrange the suitcases.

That night I could feel I was coming down with a slight fever and my stomach churned a bit. I guess the assortment of Nepalese foods cooked at a variety of homes had finally caught up with our western digestive systems. Perhaps the emotional roller coaster had also taken its toll, so I took a lot of acidophilus and some vitamins, and I hoped the physical and emotional pain would go away.

CHAPTER 35

Several devotees came early the next morning to say good-bye to Nancy. Madhavi was amongst them, and as a parting gesture Nancy decided to buy Madhavi's Krishna painting that had been displayed in the main bhajan hall. With sincere gratitude Madhavi said a prayer and vibhuti appeared on the sparkly image of a beautifully dressed Krishna playing his flute.

I said my good-byes and remained inside the puja room. But some of the others, including the Adhikaris, stayed with Nancy until she was safely situated in the cab. Even at this point the Adhikaris were exhibiting the same hands on care that they had shown throughout our Kathmandu journey. Once the cab had departed the farewell party returned to the bhajan hall and bhajans began.

Because of my physical condition Bharosha Ma decided I would not eat outside of their home during the rest of my stay. During lunch, to help settle my stomach, she encouraged me to eat a little eggplant and rice that was a part of a larger fare. There was some discussion of Nancy's hasty departure. I gave the best explanation I could to Rameshji, Bharosha Ma and Prajwol, but it was still very difficult to explain. I wasn't sure I truly understood it myself. But by the time lunch was over I felt better.

It seemed Bharosha Ma and Rameshji kept me

closer to them that day. It could have been Nancy's absence or the increase in unrest in the city. I was somewhat frightened when I heard a violent protest against the high gas prices had broken out near Arpuna's parent's home. Tires were being burned and a man was killed.

The Adhikari's did not appear to be particularly unnerved even when Asha said she had to alter her usual route to their house because of rioting. I felt comforted knowing Rameshji was closely monitoring the situation through radio, the newspaper and the plethora of devotees who seemed to know where the hotspots were. Apurna even went shopping that day and with her excellent taste in tikas/bindis gifted me with an amazing collection of the decorative face jewelry.

One of the best gifts I received was a phone call from Larry. It was so good to hear his voice. Once again I tried to explain why Nancy was on her way back to the States, with some success. But then I launched into how I would be traveling to India by myself. My emotions were on my sleeve when I spoke about it, and I could feel a bit of sadness and fear. But Larry assured me, being the world traveler that he is, that I had made all the right arrangements and that I would be fine. I don't know if he truly believed that or felt I needed to hear it in order for me to believe it. But in the end, I surrendered it all. I asked Baba for his help and protection and I put my fear back in my pocket.

The room felt somewhat lonely that night without Nancy. I looked over at her empty bed and thought about what had transpired. It felt like I had run a marathon over the last two days. I thought about something Sarit told me months before. Nobody goes to see the Avatar without his permission. He spoke of how trips had been cancelled and people who had reached India but left under one circumstance or another without going to the ashram and seeing Sathya Sai Baba. That thought dominated my mind as I fell into an exhausted sleep.

I awoke feeling refreshed the next morning. There was nothing about the day that was unusual until I sat down on the floor for morning bhajans and an invigorated Madhavi came and sat beside me.

"Mommie told me Baba was here last night."

"He was?" I probed her bright eyes.

"Yes. And he told Mommie the paintings that you and Nancy are taking back to America will help me sell more of my paintings."

I don't recall how I responded to that, but I do recall thinking how no one had told me that Sai Baba had been in the house that night. I had spoken to Bharosha Ma, but she hadn't said a word. My mind grappled with the thought of Sai Baba walking in the Adhikari's home while I was there. It grappled with the possibility.

Bhajans proceeded as usual but Madhavi, Asha, Jyoti and Kiran Uncle stayed afterwards because the shrines in the main puja room and the Goddess Temple were going to be cleaned. There was a moment in the midst of the activity that I was able to look at Bharosha Ma and say, "Baba was here?" I pointed toward the ground.

"Yes," she stated emphatically.

I turned to Rameshji and asked him to ask Bharosha Ma if she would tell me the entire account later on, while I took notes. He asked her. Bharosha Ma smiled at me and nodded, yes.

The thought of Baba being in the house was never far from my mind from that moment on, but I managed to focus on what was unfolding around me. While preparations for the cleaning were being made another woman who had attended bhajans told me her history of heart problems until she received some healings from Bharosha Ma. With what I assumed were family members standing nearby she assured me now she was just fine.

Finally when most of the devotees were gone, I watched as all of the items were removed from the altar in the main bhajan hall. There were so many of them, and the entire process took hours. Bharosha Ma and Madhavi washed a large quantity of them in a large, deep tin pan. Others were wiped down with a dry cloth and replaced. Statues of Krishna and Shirdi Sai Baba that were adorned with cloth received new cloth coverings, as did a large chair for Sai Baba and the chair where Shirdi Sai Baba sat.

There was much talk in Nepali that I didn't understand. But I knew the cleaning and other preparations were being made for Rama Navami, the celebration of Rama's birthday. As usual, Rameshji was a fountain of knowledge and always so willing to share.

He focused his efforts on a small, silver Durga statue that was surrounded by Shakti powder. It sat in a marvelously ornate silver container. A red beaded gold necklace, similar to the one Bharosha Ma gave me from Saraswati, was wrapped around the Goddess.

The silver container sat on top of a round silver platter that was totally covered with the vibrant orange Shakti powder mixed with vibhuti. There, within the combination of powders, sat a tiny pair silver padukas.

"This statue and the sandals were manifested by Baba," Rameshji explained.

Then the look dawned in his eyes that always came

before he said something extraordinary.

"Sometimes they walk around within the powder."

I looked at the tiny sandals and I could see, perhaps, eight tiny footprints in the powder. The footprints formed a vertical line extending from the container where Bhagavati sat and it looked like someone had been walking in the tiny shoes.

"I have seen them walk," Rameshji said. "And perhaps if you are deserving of seeing a miracle you will too. It depends on you." He spoke as he compacted the Shakti powder and vibhuti into a smooth somewhat lighter orange surface. "Your trust. Your comfort level."

We waited for a matter of minutes but I knew in my heart that I still found some of the things so fantastical that I harbored doubt. Although the majority of me believed what I had been experiencing, what I had seen, there still was an inkling of doubt. By now, I didn't want it to be that way, it simply was, and Rameshji's statement of, "If you are deserving of seeing a miracle," sat like a stone in my heart. I knew I did not have absolute faith and the tiny, silver sandals did not move.

The cleaning ended perhaps an hour later. Everyone had left the room except for Madhavi and me when all of a sudden she began to point at the altar.

"Chaap! Chaap!"

I had no idea what she was saying. Usually Madhavi was very careful to speak English because she wanted me to understand. She had served as an excellent interpreter throughout the trip. But in her excitement over the manifestation she forgot that I did not understand Nepali. My eyes searched the entire altar looking for the cause of her excitement.

"What is it?!" I asked.

"*Chaap!* Handprint!" Madhavi said.

I looked at Sai Baba's chair that was situated behind several objects of worship, including an unusual small, brass statue of Sai Baba. On the plum colored silk brocade cover were two handprints.

Quickly, Madhavi left through the back door. I could see she was telling the few people who remained what had just occurred.

I looked at the hand imprints again, and I just stood there. I was thinking how, unlike Madhavi who actually saw the entire process of the imprint coming in, because of my skepticism I was only allowed to see the handprints after they came. At least that's how I saw it. But in the end I thought I had been there in the room when it happened. I was there and for that moment it was enough.

CHAPTER 36

Around 1 p.m., after lunch, a small group of us, Rameshji, Madhavi, Asha, Jyoti, Apurna, Konchee, Kiran Uncle and me gathered in the main bhajan hall. We came together to hear Bharosha Ma tell about her visit with Sai Baba.

Armed with a pen and my journal I was eager and ready, but there was another thought that lurked in my mind. It concerned Bharosha Ma's composure. I was keenly aware of how serene and perhaps for lack of a better word, everyday, Bharosha Ma appeared to be despite the significant event. Her self-control made me wonder about the depth and breadth of her inner life. How much had Bharosha Ma experienced? Were there things during her night time travels with Sathya Sai Baba, a Purna Avatar, that Bharosha Ma had witnessed but were impossible for the human mind to comprehend? Things that would even challenge our imaginations? Because I can tell you, as she sat in a beautiful yellow sari trimmed in forest green and began to speak about how Sai Baba came to the house the night before, a luminescence engulfed her. There was dynamism in her eyes and on her face that I had never...never seen before.

"A bright white light descends down on me," Bharosha Ma began. "I wake up and Baba is there. He greets me with the one hand blessing and tells me He is hungry. Baba knows there is roti left from when Ramesh told me not to take bread-and-butter earlier that day.

I take Baba to the kitchen. We both eat a piece of roti and He drinks black tea. When we are done eating, we go to my bedroom and Baba blesses Ramesh. I ask Baba if Ramesh can have darshan, but Baba says it is not time yet. Then we went to Gwyn's bedroom. Baba blesses her. He tells me when she comes to Bangalore He will come very close to her and give her what she needs through His eyes. I ask about Nancy. Baba says it was his will that she not come to India, and He was instrumental in her decision to return to the States.

Then we went down to the puja room and Baba advised me about a good devotee, Asha."

At this point Rameshji did not tell me what the advice was during his interpretation. The advice may have been shared with the others in Nepali or Bharosha Ma simply did not share Asha's advice with the group because she had already talked to Asha in private.

Rameshji began to interpret for Bharosha Ma again.

"Next Baba spoke of Madhavi's paintings of Krishna. He said that Gwyn would take hers back to America and help Madhavi sell paintings in the States. Baba told me to tell Madhavi to paint on cloth so it would be easier for Gwyn to carry. Swami also told Madhavi to rub Gaurab down with a specific oil while lying in the sun. At the same time Baba told her to stretch out his limbs and he will get stronger."

I feel I must explain who Gaurab is. Gaurab is Madhavi's son and this is how he became her son. Gaurab's biological mother left him at his step mother's house one day. Through an act of anger that involved her husband and the biological mother, she threw the baby, Gaurab, out of the window. His back broke. Some neighborhood children picked Gaurab up off of the ground and took him to their house. It was from there that Madhavi took possession of Gaurab and became his mother. At the time of my visit Gaurab was about 11 years old and bound to a wheel chair. He could not talk or feed himself, but his eyes spoke worlds.

After Bharosha Ma spoke of Madhavi and Gaurab she interrupted her account about Baba's visit that previous and she recounted another visit.

"Ramesh had lost his job and I didn't know how we would make it. So I cried to Baba. 'What are we going to do Swami with no money?' Then both Sathya Sai Baba and Shirdi Sai Baba came together to the house and told me not to cry."

"People think God is in control of the devotee but in truth Baba says the devotee is in control of God," Rameshji commented before a Bharosha Ma continued her account of the night before.

"I was so excited that Baba was here that I wanted to continue to make conversation with Him." Bharosha Ma said, laughing shyly. "So I said, instead of making rice for Ram Navami I am planning to cook bread. But Baba said cooking bread was more work, more tedious to make, so it would be best to do rice.

We go outside thru the back door of the puja room and Baba states that Kiran Uncle was right about a construction error of 2 ½ inches involving a window leveling. Baba also brings up painting a very visible high part of the new construction of the house gold. He asks me why this has not been done yet. Then we walked to the front gate, and Baba disappears."

After Bharosha Ma finished her account the conversation continued in Nepali, and while they talked I was absorbed by thoughts of Bharosha Ma saying Sai Baba had come to my bedroom. That the Avatar had come to my bedroom, blessed me, and said when I got to India that he would give me what I needed through his eyes. It was a major energetic injection in what was already a mystical, amazing experience in Kathmandu. It was this wonderful bombshell.

But while I sat there thinking, Kiran Uncle got up and left the group very quickly when some of the construction crew returned from what I assumed was a lunch break. Through a window I watched him approach a particular man. He brought him over to the window and motioned as if he was explaining what Bharosha Ma said Sai Baba had said the night before; that there was some kind of problem with the window. The construction crew member took out a measuring tool, took a measurement, and the next thing I see are nods of agreement between the two men.

Rameshji left and basically the group dispersed, but I followed Bharosha Ma, Madhavi and Asha to the Goddess Temple where they began to clean the temple and redress the Goddesses.

It was so incredible to watch Madhavi and Asha. First they removed beautiful, fine, red nets with sparkly enhancements of gold and other colors from the Goddesses heads and therefore their faces. Next an assortment of jewelry that included bangles, necklaces and hair ornaments came off, and then, finally, human sized saris.

The Goddesses were in seated poses and sat perhaps three feet tall. Lakshmi wore a green sari. Durga's sari was red, and Saraswati's was blue. When their saris were removed there was a profuse amount of the bright orange powder on their bodies, but I noticed Durga had more than Lakshmi and Saraswati. A large portion of the Shakti powder also fell to the temple floor as a result of the undressing. I longed to scoop up a small amount and take it with me, but I knew that would not be the proper thing to do. So after a few minutes I mustered up the courage and I asked Bharosha Ma if I could have some of the manifested powder.

As and answer to my question, Bharosha Ma's eyes ignited and she looked at me for a prolonged moment. Then I watched her remove some of the Shakti powder directly from Durga's body before she took several of Saraswati's blue bangles, and that is what she gave to me.

Through it all Madhavi and Asha continued to work. They readjusted the strands of beads that hung around the Goddesses throats, and the gold that dangled from the tops of their heads onto their foreheads so that it lay directly against their third eye. Next they added more bangles, mostly red and gold. I watched, totally impressed, as they folded and pleated the elegant saris until they fit the Goddesses demure frames, before they draped a fresh set of red nets trimmed in gold fringe over their heads. On top of that they layered an even heavier, more elaborate version of the netting. Finally Asha and Madhavi were done. The Goddesses were adorned beyond compare. Gayatri was redressed and I helped, in whatever small fashion I could, them clean and tidy the remainder of the temple.

Later that day I noticed more than a dozen women had gathered on the lawn near the entrance of the Adhikari's property. As they sat on two massive red rugs the collective colors of saris and sawal kameez were beautiful in the bright sunshine. I don't know how long they had been there, but it must have been awhile. I watched as they chatted, peeled and cut up some of the vegetables that would feed the people who attended Rama Navami the next day.

Heaps of cauliflower and potatoes were piled high on round, flat, woven trays and in large bowls and pots; while copious amounts of vegetables in plastic bags, and an empty rug, waited nearby. Based on that empty rug I assumed before the day was over that more women would join them.

Throughout the day preparations were being made and there was a larger than average crowd at bhajans that evening. Once while I was standing near Bharosha Ma she told a female devotee, who interpreted for me, that in the future I would have Baba's grace. It was at those moments more than any other that I wished I could talk directly to Bharosha Ma. Just like I wished she could have come to me and told me that Baba had blessed me in my room.

After dinner that night Rameshji talked of how Baba always instructed them to feed the people during certain religious festivals, and inevitably large crowds showed up. Rameshji wasn't sure how large the crowd would be for Rama's birthday because Nepali New Year was being celebrated in two days, and normally Rama Navami was not celebrated in such a huge fashion.

The day was done and I was about to retire to my room, so I said my goodnights.

"Gwyn." Rameshji stopped me. "I want to tell you something before you go to bed."

"Yes."

"Baba told Bharosha that when you come to India he will give you what you need through his eyes."

"Yes, I recall that."

There was a knowing in Rameshji's eyes when he spoke again. "The most powerful way that Baba transmits his energy is through his eyes."

"Is it?"

"Yes. It is."

I went to bed that night thinking about it, and wondering how his energy would affect my life, and what it meant to have Sai Baba's grace.

That night, I saw the silver, manifested Durga touch my forehead in a dream.

CHAPTER 37

I got up early, before 6:30 that next morning, dressed for Rama Navami and went down to the main bhajan hall. Baba's footprints had materialized on the silk brocade runner in front of Shirdi Sai Baba's chair, and the tiny silver sandals had also "walked" in the tray beneath the materialized silver Durga statue. The tiny footprints were very obvious in the Shakti powder.

When Rameshji joined me he counted twelve of them.

"This is a very good sign," he said. "Based on my experiences, the greater the number of small footprints the more auspicious the occasion will be."

Shortly thereafter Bharosha Ma joined us.

"Bharosha is going to do puja with the flower tray beneath the materialized Shiva lingam," he announced.

I assumed this was a ritual Bharosha Ma performed before every festival. So as she prepared for puja, suddenly, I became so chilled that I had to have another shawl.

"I'll be right back," I said not able to sit there any longer.

I ran upstairs as quickly as I could, but when I got there a kind of monkey mind set in. I could not decide which shawl to wear, and when I finally returned downstairs Bharosha Ma's puja was over and she had left the bhajan hall. Rameshji on the other hand was on his way out.

I looked at the Shiva lingam and saw the flower had jumped on top of it. Several other flowers also adorned the altar. Again Rameshji's comment, "If you are deserving of seeing a miracle depends on you," echoed in my head. Instinctively, I knew my becoming chilled was no coincidence, that the speck of doubt I possessed, no matter how small, was a definite hindrance to my flat out witnessing Bharosha Ma's puja, and therefore my seeing the flower jump on top of the lingam.

I also thought about how Sai Baba told Bharosha Ma, during his visit, that he was instrumental in Nancy's decision to return to the States. I knew he was instrumental in my needing a shawl.

Somewhat disappointed that I had not seen the manifestation of the jumping flower I exited through the backdoor of the puja room. When I emerged outside I saw Madhavi standing inside the Goddess Temple. I went over and joined her.

Immediately, she smiled. "Sai Ram."

"Sai Ram," I replied.

"I did a Durga puja this morning," Madhavi said, "and a Baba puja. Then I asked Swami for a message. I offered this cucumber." Madhavi picked up the vegetable that lay on the temple floor between Lakshmi and Durga. She began to read. "Madhavi, you have done a good Durga puja, and puja to me." She showed me the Hindi writing. From the look on her face Madhavi's pleasure from receiving a message from Sai Baba was absolute.

The message was wonderful, but there was something else in the Goddess temple that absolutely astounded me. Madhavi had locked up the temple the night before as she did every night. But today, after re-adorning the Goddesses the day before, the visible Shakti powder had increased exponentially.

Where it increased was also of interest to me. Lakshmi's mouth was totally encased in a wide patch of the substance, and there was some about her throat. On Durga's face a generous sprinkling appeared in small patches and light sprays, and more of the powder was around Durga's throat than on Lakshmi's. But it was Saraswati who had the most obvious increase in Shakti powder of all. There was some in the fold of her mouth, but the Shakti powder that had accumulated around her throat was so thick that it formed a knot on the left side of her neck, almost like a swollen gland.

I <u>knew</u> the Shakti powder had materialized on its own. I had seen the extensive work, under Bharosha Ma's supervision, that Madhavi and Asha performed the day before. There was no Shakti powder on their faces and very little around their throats when the process was done.

I marveled at a particular thought. Perhaps the essence of Goddesses had entered into the statues and became aware of the loving ministrations that had been given. And how did they react? With a profuse outpouring of Shakti, creative energy, which manifested as a bright, orange powder.

"They think we are turning God into statues," I was once told Sai Baba had said, "but we are turning statues into Gods."

Absolutely, far-fetched for most minds. I know.

When I returned to the main bhajan hall where audio equipment was being set up, Rameshji informed me Sujata had called. Nancy had arrived safely in the

United States and was staying at the Rimals.

During the Rama Navami, I felt I witnessed lives of true service and work in full gear. I had seen some of it in Salt Lake City but this was a whole new level. I don't know what time the cooking began, but by lunch time huge pots of cauliflower and potatoes, curried egg-plant, steamed rice and a sweet rice dessert were being served on a long table near a hedge, that bordered one side of the Adhikari's front lawn. Approximately 500 people, maybe a little more ate that day, including the employees of a carpet factory, who could see from the rooftop where they worked how the event was progressing. They came to eat when the food was ready. They left after they had eaten.

Expansive, blue tarps covered several areas of the front lawn, and people ate and talked where ever they could. A line of participants snaked through the yard and around the house before they reached the servers, and once they had their plates they sat out in the open, or under palm trees, or on the top of the flat wall. Those who could not find a seat stood.

Special applications of cum cum and rice and some applications of black charcoal were applied to our fore-heads, and a bracelet made of yellow thread was tied on one of our wrists by an elderly man of the community.

Once the food had been eaten an early afternoon session of bhajans was held. Because of the speakers which had been set up earlier, the singing could be heard throughout the yard and into the second bhajan hall be-hind the Goddess Temple.

After bhajans, special balls of cotton strung with camphor bits were lit. It was an absolutely full day. When it was over, various devotees pitched in to clean up. If my memory serves me right, bhajans were still held that evening, but only a small core group of devotees attended.

I was tired. I could only imagine that most of the people who participated and helped with Rama Navami were as well. Before I went to bed that night talk of Bharosha Ma flying with me to India surfaced again. I believe she was concerned about my traveling alone. To have Bharosha Ma travel with me to see Sai Baba would have been the ultimate as I see it now, and even as I saw it back then, but I determined however my journey to India unfolded, I would be okay.

CHAPTER 38

The day before my last day in Kathmandu had arrived, and the surreal quality of everything I had experienced since meeting the Adhikaris had not lessened one bit. As I sang bhajans that morning, thinking that after tomorrow I may not see Rameshji and Bharosha Ma under those circumstances again, that I may never see the people I had become so fond of like Lily, Siru, Madhavi, Apurna, Prajwol and Asha, the experiences we shared became that much more dreamlike.

I had spent 22 weeks with the Adhikaris, and as I sang the bhajan 'Say The Name of Sathya Sai' I thought about the Avatar who had resurrected Bharosha Ma and thereby created my remarkable journey. I was convinced that Sathya Sai Baba was just what he was reported to be, a Purna Avatar, and that all the manifestations around Bharosha Ma were as real as I was. No, I did not understand the how of it, but that didn't change the truth.

As I finished singing, a flower dropped down to the altar. It was a blossom from a lei that had been draped across the top of the large, vibhuti filled photograph of Sai Baba; the photo that dominated the wall behind the shrine. Immediately a devotee picked the blossom up and gave it to me.

"When a flower falls during a bhajan like that," she whispered, "Baba is blessing the person who is singing."

Several women nearby concurred with nods.

So I took the flower.

"Thank you," I said, already teary eyed, and I pressed the flower between the pages of my bhajan book, as I had seen Sujata do with the blossoms Baba had twisted into her hair the night she slept with her mother in her Salt Lake puja room.

After morning bhajans I packed a few items but there were several errands on my plate. So I secured Indian rupees, confirmed my plane ticket, and shopped with Apurna for shawls that I would hand out as gifts when I returned to the States.

There was no further mention of Bharosha Ma traveling with me, so I knew I would be going alone. But Bharosha Ma and Apurna stayed in my room that night until my suitcase was packed and I went to bed.

That next morning life was on fast forward. Rameshji explained how a protest was anticipated, and if I didn't leave for the airport earlier than we had intended, I might not be able to leave that day.

Bharosha Ma gave me a hug and a hair ornament that came from Durga as a parting gift, and I was hustled toward a car that waited in the street outside the Adhikari's wall.

A small group of devotees that included Madhavi gathered with other members of the Adhikari family to say farewell. The goodbyes were difficult as good byes can be, and I am not one who can easily hold back tears. So I cried a little as I promised not to forget anyone who had touched my heart, and hoped those whose hearts I had touched would not forget me.

Rameshji who is never at a loss had some last words of advice.

"Do not cry. This is not a sad time. You are going to India to see the Avatar. When you get there do not dictate to God what he should do, and please, call us when you arrive in Bangalore. Let us know how you are doing."

With those parting words my cab pulled away and I was on the third leg of my journey.

A male devotee accompanied me to the airport and my check-in was extremely smooth. As I sat in the plane on the tarmac, thinking about my three weeks in Nepal and waiting for the plane to pull away from the gate, an airport employee in a sharp uniform came down the aisle. I could tell he was a man with some authority.

"Are you Gwyn? He asked.

"Yes, I am." I replied, thinking that I had seen him before.

"I know that you were a guest of Bharosha's and Ramesh. I simply wanted to make sure that you had gotten on the plane safely."

"Yes, I have," I said. "Thank you, so much for asking."

"It is my pleasure." He gave a pronounced nod. "I will let them know that you are fine and about to take off to India." He smiled. "Sai Ram. Have a pleasant trip."

"Sai Ram," I replied.

I watched him walk back up the aisle and disappear from my view. Moments later the doors were secured and the plane backed away from the gate. I said good-bye to Nepal.

CHAPTER 39

After a smooth customs check I emerged from the Bangalore Airport, walked a few yards, and as I had been promised a Babu Cab Company driver was holding up a sign with my name on it. That was a comfort. We greeted each other, loaded up the cab and headed out of the airport. I felt myself relax even more as we passed a gigantic photograph of Sathya Sai Baba welcoming visitors to the city.

"My name is Abdul, madam," he told me as he drove. "I will be your driver for the duration of your stay."

"That's good to know," I replied.

"You are staying at the Sai Renaissance Hotel, madam?"

"Yes, I am."

"It is a nice hotel. I know it well. I will take you there right away."

I thanked him again and we were on our way.

From what I could see of downtown Bangalore it was basically clean and lush. It was quite different from what Larry had experienced on some of his business trips to India and from the images I'd seen on the Travel Channel and National Geographic, different from the chaotic, almost overpowering environment of Mumbai and New Delhi. Still, as we drove, I became very aware of India's status as a Third World country. But like Nepal, the colors of the women's clothing provided an uplifting element to what were obviously destitute areas.

It didn't take long to arrive at the Sai Renaissance in Whitefield. I checked in, put my belongings in my room and took a three wheeled cab to Brindavan, Sai Baba's summer home and ashram. I was surprised that it was so close; no more than a quarter of a mile directly up the street.

My timing couldn't have been better; visitors were being maneuvered into several lines and seated for *darshan*, the seeing of a holy person, the Avatar.

I was put in a long queue of women before I finally ended up sitting with I don't know how many women in a section outside of a very large, covered structure. We sat for quite some time before music began, and eventually Sathya Sai Baba appeared at the edge of the covered structure. There he stood in his orange robe at the top of several stairs that lead down to the open space where a vast number of us sat.

Sai Baba was quite a distance away but I could see him clearly and I felt a kind of awe. He blessed us with his right open palm, but as gracefully as he appeared he disappeared into the covered area. Afterwards as the music continued to play, I experienced peaceful waves of energy that were unmistakable and lasted for several minutes, and when it ended the Avatar delivered a discourse on the Gayatri mantra.

Before I left the ashram that day I enquired about Sai Baba's daily schedule. I was told darshan was held at 7 or 7:30 in the morning and the gates opened at 4:50 a.m. Bhajans were held at four in the afternoon. I was advised it would be a very good idea to arrive early in order to get a somewhat decent seat.

Arrive early??? I didn't know how much good arriving early would do when I was certain all 30,000 of us had the same desire. That's how many people I was told was at Brindavan, more than 30,000 visitors.

I suddenly recalled how Bharosha Ma had told me the day before I left that "Baba, Bangalore." In other words, up until that day Sai Baba had been in Puttaparthi. Brindavan was much smaller than the ashram in Puttaparthi, which had hosted more than 1 million people for Sai Baba's 75th birthday.

When I left the ashram I found a place where I could make international phone calls. First I called Larry and told him I had arrived safely. Next I attempted to speak with the Adhikaris but their phone line was busy, so feeling exhausted I returned to the hotel, took a shower and went to bed.

I rose early the next morning and joined an established line of women outside the ashram gates. In both directions a host of vendors selling Sathya Sai Baba photos, statuettes of Hindu gods, CD's, DVD's and jewelry, lined the street in front of Brindavan. Even at 4:30 a.m., a vendor played soft musical mantras accompanied by morning birdsongs, a fitting backdrop for the unique, dark scene and sleepy seekers like me.

Finally, the gates opened. When I entered the ashram I was directed toward a particular line. This time I was seated right outside of the covered area. Sai Baba was in viewing range but he was very far away. Still I enjoyed the darshan and the musicians who played for the Avatar.

I went to Puttaparthi that afternoon. I wanted to see 'Prashanti Nilayam', 'The Abode of Supreme Peace", Baba's first ashram, created in the southern city where he was born. I couldn't have asked for a better driver and guide, and I inwardly thanked Connie Shaw for her recommendation. Abdul answered questions or engaged in conversation only when I initiated the exchange. His professional, "Yes, madam," or "No, madam," enhanced my positive feeling about India.

It was a two and a half hour drive. The Avatar's influence was apparent as we drew near to the outskirts of the hot, southern city where the homes and businesses appeared to be more prosperous.

On the way we passed a massive edifice with amazing architecture that contrasted starkly against the rough countryside.

"What is that?" I asked Abdul.

"It is Sai Baba's Super Specialty Hospital, madam."

"So this is the Super Specialty Hospital, "I replied.

"Yes, madam. Sai Baba has built two hospitals. That one, and a general hospital in Bangalore. Services are free to the public, madam."

I stared at the building. This is the place where Bharosha Ma was pronounced dead, I thought as it disappeared from sight.

When Prashanti Nilayam could be seen in the distance, the nearby Indian homes were painted in pastel blues, pinks and yellows. As I walked a small portion of the ashram property, it was too hot to do more, the same pastels were prevalent on the exterior of the university and other buildings, as well as the huge statues that reigned over the property. Prashanti Nilayam reminded me of a large, artistic college campus nestled in the midst of a small, bustling town; bustling because of the university's presence.

During the next two days I went to Brindavan twice a day, always taking a short nap in between. Each time

I was placed in queue lines where I ended up with a seat outside of the covered area.

The next morning I thought I had gotten lucky, and I had. My line was directed under the massive roof, but I was only rows from the back and from the outside where I had sat during my entire stay.

By then I had become very aware of two other lines. The women in those lines were lead away from the masses, of which I was one, and were seated in the middle section of the covered area. I longed to be in those lines, but I didn't know who those women were and how they merited closer seats.

The following evening when I left my outdoor seat, I was informed that the festival was over and that the crowds would thin substantially from 30,000 to perhaps 12,000. It was interesting news but I hadn't known there was a festival, and I didn't see how that would make a difference in where I was being seated.

As I walked back to my hotel I thought of how Bharosha Ma had walked near me in my home that day and said, "This is how Sai Baba will be looking at you." I had no idea how that would ever happen when I was seated so far away.

I climbed into bed and took my usual nap, but that day I dreamed of Bharosha Ma and Sai Baba, although I could not remember the details.

By that time, I'd made a habit of taking practically every meal at the Sai Renaissance Restaurant. That evening when I went for dinner, I was surprised to see Ted Henry, the ABC reporter who I met at the Rimal's, and his wife, Jody. Naturally, I went over and spoke to them. They were finishing their meal, but they wanted to hear about my trip to Kathmandu, so I sat with them while my food was being prepared.

Ted told me Baba had promised them an interview a couple of days before, but it never happened. The interviews that Sai Baba held were actually prized personal meetings with various devotees. Because the interview did not take place, the Henrys made a decision to stay two more days with hopes that it still might. When I saw them they had resigned themselves to the fact that they were not going to get an interview with the Avatar during this visit. The told me they would be boarding a flight back to the States in the morning.

But they had gotten close enough to Sai Baba to request an interview and I wondered how. So I asked them. Ted's status as a reporter was the main reason, but in the end, because I was writing a book on Bharosha Ma, and because of my journalistic approach to my trip Jody and another woman who dined with them gave me a name.

CHAPTER 40

When I entered Brindavan at 5 a.m. the next day, I asked for that woman. After being directed several places I finally found her, but was disappointed to hear her say she had nothing to do with seating. She wanted to know who had given me her name... and that is why I am withholding it in this memoir.

Yet and still she presented me to the woman in charge. We talked for a moment, and the next thing I knew I was placed in what I called the 2nd waiting line. This *seva dal,* which means ashram helper, made a place for me in that line and I couldn't believe my good fortune. I stood there taking it all in when the woman behind me said, "We have been waiting a long time for you."

Even in the midst of my excitement, I thought that was a very strange thing for her to say. But my sudden change in seating status, and the early morning hour had me somewhat dazed, so I simply gave her a broad smile. But as I write this now I wonder why a total stranger would make such a comment.

After this miraculous journey I have my thoughts about it, but as a reader who has stayed with me to this point of my memoir I will allow you to draw your own conclusions.

Soon a seva dal motioned for my line to move toward the covered area. When we reached the platform the line split. Some women were led to a center section, but I was led to the front section.

I was next in line to be seated and the seva dal asked in the kindest of voices, "Will the second row be okay?"

Stunned, I replied, "Whatever you think is acceptable." But as she led me to my seat my heart absolutely sang.

She indicated a mat and I sat down. I was in the second row!

In front of me was a walkway, and on the other side of that another section of women were seated in rows that were perhaps ten deep. I looked behind them at a stage that was maybe 40 ft away.

There were several objects on the stage, but what I remember most was a magnificently decorated large chair. It was Sathya Sai Baba's chair, and I thought of the chairs I had seen in the Adhikari's and Rimal's puja rooms.

Soon a red and blue carpet runner was rolled out on all of the walkways, and several seva dals came forward and wiped it off with dry cloths. They also made sure it was smooth and seamless while others dusted the floor near the runner.

For approximately 45 minutes I sat unable to believe my good fortune, when all of a sudden I got a glimpse of Sai Baba. He was waiting to enter the bhajan hall and appeared to be standing alone.

Moments later music filled the air and Baba walked out, followed closely by six men dressed in white. He walked slowly, surveying the people near the entrance. At first it appeared that Swami was going to walk down another runway, then suddenly He took the one in front of me!

As He advanced He focused His attention on the

people on the opposite side of the walkway, but as Baba drew closer he turned to my side. He took a letter from one woman. Then He stopped and talked with another who sat beside the woman sitting directly in front of me. I have no idea what language they spoke because I was gazing so intently at his face. Even if they had been speaking English I don't know if I would have understood.

Beautiful! I thought. Absolutely beautiful! That's how I saw His face. At 76 years of age Sathya Sai Baba's skin was as clear as a baby's skin. Then, just for a split-second, he glanced at me and I saw his eyes, dark and large, before He continued to speak to His devotee with soft yet animated expressions. The next thing I knew He continued on His way.

Baba walked through the women's section and the men's section, choosing various walkways, taking many letters and every once in awhile giving the blessing sign. It was the longest darshan I had experienced since I had arrived.

I left darshan in a state of joy and with a remarkable sense of peace. I couldn't believe my good fortune, my blessing, to see and experience the Avatar at such a close range!

Before I left, I bought several books from the ashram bookstore and bumped into a woman from Little Rock Arkansas. She had heard of my trip to Kathmandu with Bharosha Ma from Dr. Sunny Anand.

My sleep that afternoon was so deep, similar to how I had felt when I had taken some kind of prescription drug. I also experienced elusive dreams about Sai Baba and several Hindu Gods and Goddesses.

During my next trip to bhajans I was placed in the

fifth row. Afterwards I returned to my hotel, grabbed something to eat and was in the bed before 6:30. I slept through the entire night; again a drugged-like sleep.

I had an excellent seat the next day and from that day on I continued to be seated in the front section for the remainder of my stay.

It's amazing how much fruit my diligence in attending bhajans at the Rimal's house bore in India. First it was the woman who knew about my trip to Kathmandu courtesy of Dr. Sunny Anand. Next I met Diane Ness, an acquaintance of Reverend Pipes. Through Diane I visited the homes of some Sai Baba devotees who lived in India, and a few who were frequent guests from other countries, like Mayfair Agyeman, who was born in Ghana, but who currently lived in London.

One of the most memorable doors that Diane opened was an opportunity to taste amrit that was continuously manifesting from a small stone image of the Avatar. It occurred in Delsey and Desmond's apartment. The owner of the image lived in Mysore and had traveled to Bangalore to see the Avatar. He had many miracles to tell involving Sathya Sai Baba, and the amrit was the sweetest most floral substance I had ever tasted.

On two more occasions the Avatar came near to where I sat. Once He spoke to the woman directly in front of me but He never looked my way. The second time he spoke to another devotee who was seated directly in front of me, but this time He gave me a direct look. I remember His eyes were dark and probing. When He continued on his way tears formed in my eyes. I was so grateful for the experience. Grateful to be so near to Sathya Sai Baba, the Avatar. Grateful for my life.

On my last morning, I left my packed suitcases

with the concierge and attended darshan. During the break between darshan and bhajans I stayed in the ashram room of a woman from California. Her name was Baba Ra. We became acquainted in one of the queues a few days earlier. On another occasion she offered me respite in her ashram room between Baba's scheduled appearances. Thanks to her I didn't walk back to the hotel in the middle of the hot, Indian day.

Baba Ra had been staying at Baba's ashrams in India for a year and a half. On my last day she also suggested that I visit with her as I waited for my last bhajan, and that we eat our midday meal in the Western canteen.

Because it was my last day, as confirmed by the seva dal, I was seated on the front row and Baba Ra was seated behind me. This time when Sai Baba emerged, He climbed up the stairs and stood in the middle of the stage. Baba looked out at the crowd and I thought his gaze focused on me. But I didn't dare think that was true until Baba Ra leaned in and said in an excited voice, "He's looking directly at you!"

"He is looking at me!" I replied.

Baba Ra confirmed what I suspected but was too stunned to believe.

Bhajans were held and at the end Sathya Sai Baba came over and stood in front of the women's section. He raised both his hands with his palms toward us in a double blessing.

"He's doing a double blessing," Baba Ra exclaimed. "He is doing a double blessing. I've been here for a year and a half and I've never seen a double blessing. I believe it has something to do with you."

I didn't know what to say but I thought of Bharosha Ma.

We continued to watch Him. He walked across the stage and stopped in front of the men's section and repeated the mudra. Next the Avatar walked over to the stairs, descended them, and disappeared out of sight.

As I waited in the airport with an international collection of Sai Baba devotees, the fact that he had given a double blessing was the topic of conversation within several of the groups.

I couldn't help but think about what Baba Ra had said. "He is looking directly at you!"

I thought about how Bharosha Ma had looked at me in my home in Salt Lake City, her eyes probing as she said, "This is how Baba will be looking at you. How she had said Swami had blessed me in my room during his night time visit to her home in Kathmandu and said, "I will come near to her and give her what she needs through my eyes."

I can not say what Sai Baba gave me through his eyes, but I can say he came close enough to do so, and overall Bharosha Ma was right.

I thought my journey with Bharosha Ma and ultimately Sathya Sai Baba had come to an end when I arrived back in the United States. It had been quite an adventure in so many ways, and maybe my resistance was down from all the traveling and the stress that it can sometimes cause, but when I awoke the day after I arrived at home, I was coming down with a cold. So I decided to start my day with an Om Sai Prayers CD that I purchased in India, and to make myself a cup of peach tea.

As I sat in my robe and sipped on the hot drink, I reminisced about some of the things I had experienced in Kathmandu and in India. I had just a small amount of tea left, maybe a couple of inches, when I glanced into my cup. What did I see? All of the sediment from the tea leaves was in the form of a perfect ohm! Shocked was not the word!

I jumped up to look for my camera and I took some photographs. After that I called Larry and told him what had happened.

"Are you sure?" He asked.

“I am sure. It looks like the ohm Sai Baba would put on the bananas or on the fruit that you saw at Sujata and Sarit's house. But this ohm also has the line on top of it. And I mean this line is totally straight! It’s so clear there's no mistaking it for anything else.” I chuckled. “I guess it's my welcome home,” I said.

“It's your welcome ohm,” Larry said not missing a beat.

EPILOGUE

As I look back, my preparation for writing this book started a long time ago. It may have commenced with my first dream of Sathya Sai Baba in 1988. But I am certain it was in full process from the time the "Indian man" appeared in the Paris subway in 1989, and showed me the exact same ring that was manifested by the Avatar for Rameshji Adhikari. This book was being formed back then; exotic location writing career and all.

Nancy...Genshin was right. I was being prepared for a role in Bharosha Ma's life. I was the one who would write this story, supported by Bharosha Ma's intent fusing of my connection with Saraswati, the Goddess of knowing and the arts.

I must note that Genshin's trip to Kathmandu, in my opinion, helped her go to the depths of Zen. It was the first leg of a challenging journey. Shortly after Genshin returned to the United States she discovered she had a brain tumor. She went through two arduous trials of brain surgery, and with an amazing recovery she has established the Kannon-Ji Zen Temple in Bilsborrow, West United Kingdom.

But this is also important. Nancy informed me during one of our visits while she was still in the United States and I was still in Salt Lake City, that for some reason or another she had her foot x-rayed. During that process the medical technician noticed that at some point her big toe had been broken. The technician also said it had been set perfectly (by Bharosha Ma), and had healed without any problems.

There was a remarkable thing that happened while I was writing this book. On March 10, 2009, I called Bharosha Ma and Rameshji. I spoke to Mommie briefly. We shared a sincere exchange of "I love yous," before she handed the phone to Rameshji. During that conversation Rameshji asked me something he had never asked in the seven years I had known him.

"Are you having any experiences with God?"

"What?" The question caught me off guard.

"Are you having any experiences with God?" He repeated.

At the time I thought... no.

Although I felt the question was significant I ignored that intuitive feeling and I reached for an answer. I told Rameshji I'd had some dreams with Bharosha Ma, one of them was a healing, and a few months earlier I experienced what I felt was a significant dream with Sathya Sai Baba. Before I went to bed that night I thought about the question again, and because of writing this memoir, I thought about the times Sai Baba had spoken through Sarit and Rameshji.

Well, I dreamed of Sai Baba that night. In the dream he manifested a unique gold ring for me. The main portion of the ring featured three faces of Sai Baba formed in gold, and one of them was a profile. The ring also contained amethyst and purple jade.

I woke up and shared the dream with Larry, and I also called Waheedah and told her. She was proving to be a wonderful support system through my writing process.

After that I sat down and wrote for while, but I had errands to run that day and I needed to get started.

I went into the bathroom to prepare for a shower and I looked into the mirror. The skin between my eyebrows where the third eye is situated looked different. And that's when I saw it. I saw an ohm like the ones that had manifested on the bananas and in my teacup (without the line) in my third eye. It was an ohm but it was backwards! I studied it for a minute or so to make sure I wasn't making it up. When I was absolutely convinced, I called Waheedah again. We talked about it and I realized the ohm appeared backwards to me because I was looking in the mirror. In the end Waheedah and I concluded with the Avatar, and my writing a book about Bharosha Ma, anything was possible.

It just so happened Larry came home for lunch that day, but I decided not to tell him what I thought I saw in my third eye. I decided that we would eat lunch, and before he went back to work I would just casually ask him to take a look. Once we finished eating I beckoned for him to follow me to the bathroom mirror.

"Do you see anything on my forehead?"

Larry leaned forward just a bit and quickly replied, "It looks like an ohm to me."

That did it! I laughed and said something like, "If I was going crazy I was going to be crazy by myself and not tell you what I thought I saw."

The ohm became a little darker, with the tail end of it being the darkest of all. A couple of days later my skin peeled ever so slightly around the darkest portion of the symbol. Then the entire ohm was the same tone, almost like a very light mendhi or henna.

Once again, I called Bharosha Ma and Rameshji, and

I told Rameshji about the dream and the ohm. It was interesting because, when I reminded Rameshji that he had asked me, twice, the question, “Are you having any experiences with God?” he hesitated before he replied, and I felt as if he didn't remember saying it. When Rameshji did reply, he validated my suspicion. He said, "That was Baba who was speaking to you."

Over the next ten days the ohm became lighter and lighter. During that time I contemplated, deeply, why did the Avatar send that particular energy, although I knew it was totally connected with this book about Bharosha Ma. Actually, it was the second time Sai Baba had sent a manifestation that was connected with my work. Remember when Bharosha Ma, Rameshji and the Rimal’s visited my home in Salt Lake City? Vibhuti appeared on my computer as a visible blessing of my work, in other words this memoir, and I believe the ohm that he placed in my third eye was sent to help me write insightfully about Bharosha Adhikari.

On several occasions Rameshji told me Sai Baba said Bharosha was Mother Earth, and he also referred to her as Sita on the divine fax. Many times as I wrote this memoir a question surfaced. Why Bharosha? Why this particular female body? Now, in association with some of the things I was told about Bharosha Ma’s life, I’ll briefly summarize some of the insights that came to me.

Bharosha Ma was conceived and born in Nepal, the same country as the original Sita, after Bharosha Ma’s mother, Liladevi, had experienced a miscarriage. The miscarried baby had been a girl, and there was negative talk in the community after such an inauspicious occurrence. Distraught, she went to the Ganges River to offer her prayers to the Goddess.

Now, in actuality, Liladevi, traveled to the Kamala River, located in the Janakpur District of Nepal. The Kamala River is one of the tributaries of the Ganges because it flows into the Bhurengi, which flows into the Kosi, which flows into the Mother River, Ganges. It is important to note that the Kamala River flows through the land where the original Sita was discovered in a furrow (Sita means furrow, cleft) by her father the King of Mithila. Mithila is present day Janakpur. In other words, Bharosha Ma's mother prayed on the land where the original Sita was unearthed.

Liladevi went into the Kamala River and asked with all her life's energy to have another daughter. After performing such a prayer Bharosha Ma was conceived and born. Liladevi says after delivering her daughter with no pain, she knew Bharosha was a boon from Parvati, which is another name for Lakshmi, Vishnu's consort.

This is another important marker. At eight or nine years old, as I have written, Bharosha Ma retrieved a golden statue of a five faced Vishnu from an opening in the earth...a furrow, thereby establishing another link with Sita. Sita is considered to be an incarnation of Vishnu's consort, Lakshmi by some, and an incarnation of his wife Bhudevi, Mother Earth, by others. Sathya Sai Baba is an incarnation in a series of Avatars that commenced with Vishnu and includes Rama, the spouse of the original Sita.

In Hinduism it is known that an Avatar (male) never incarnates without his Avatara (female), and although Sathya Sai Baba is known to be both Shiva/male and Shakti/female, I believe when he brought Bharosha back to life he manifested another aspect of His Shakti as Bharosha Ma.

I will end this last segment with a portion of a recorded telephone interview with Rameshji. It was a part of a series of interviews that I conducted during my attempts to tie up some loose ends for this book.

"The night visits," I said, "...when Baba actually comes to the house at night, how long has that been going on, Rameshji?"

"We have...5 or 6 times He has come, but not only at night. It has happened in the daytime also. The day time visit was very long. It was about 12 o'clock in the afternoon. That day Bharosha's sister, Bunu was, there and Suchita was there. They had some plans to buy some head covers or something like that, and they went up to my room as they were going out, and they saw Bharosha was talking to, they thought some mailman."

I laughed.

"And they thought oh, this is very simple, you know. Didi (which is a respectful term for sister) is talking, and they didn't want to disturb her. So they went on their way and shopped, and they passed about one hour, and they returned after buying what they wanted. When they came back they see the man was still talking with her, and they had some fear about this. The man had been talking for more than an hour. So they peeped the room, since it was daytime, and then they saw Baba was sitting, and Bharosha was sitting there talking. It was Baba to whom she was sitting there talking, even before going shopping and after coming back. Baba was sitting there talking with her. And then Bunu and Suchita, they also joined the conversation.

"Oh!" I gasped. "When was that?"

"I can't give you the exact date but I can find out."

"I mean, was it this year? Or last year?"

It was four or five years ago. This is a very interesting one," Rameshji said before he continued. "And then, they also joined and they talked to Baba also. This was in the daytime." Rameshji stressed. "They talked for a few minutes, and Baba said let's go to my room. You know my room on the second floor?"

"Yes," I replied.

"While they were going to my room, Baba said he wanted to go to the bathroom."

"Yes."

"You know?"

"Yes."

"Baba.... Suchita assisted him. Baba gave a shawl to Suchita, and she stood holding it outside the bathroom door. And Baba entered there and then after a few minutes He came back, and Baba, Suchita, Bunu and Bharosha all came to my room. And there again Baba sat on the sofa and Bharosha sat in the bedroom, and they started talking. Meanwhile a telephone call came from 7 kilometer hours from my place. It is in the capital of Kathmandu's center, Kasthamandap. From there the lady called Prava, Prava Didi, she phoned. The phone was ringing and Bharosha picked up the phone and she talked to Prava, and Bharosha said, 'Would you like to talk to Baba? Baba is here nearby.' Then Prava said, 'How is...what are you talking about?' And Bharosha said I will give the receiver to Baba and you talk. Then she gave the receiver to Baba and Baba talked to Prava."

I laughed again.

'This has been published in some other magazine in Nepal. Prava Didi, she has wrote the article on it," he informed me. "And she said...Prava talked to Baba, and she said, "Hello."

"Hello."

"And she said, "'Are you Baba?'"

"And Baba said, 'Yes, I am. I am Sathya Sai speaking. Do you have anything to say?'"

"And she says, "'Yes, Baba, I have many things to say to you. I am very much worried for my son. I am worried for my husband also. And I am also very much concerned for Bharosha."

"'I am very pleased that you are concerned about Bharosha. And do you know who Bharosha is?' Baba asked her," Rameshji said.

"'I don't know,' she said."

"'Bharosha is Sita of the modern age,' Sathya Sai Baba said. 'She is the Mother of this age. You go on being concerned about Bharosha. Always think about Bharosha. It is good to hear. And good for you also.'"

* * *

Most Westerners relegate miracles to the past, but the same can not be said about the inhabitants of countries like India and Nepal. Many in those eastern lands accept miracles as an every day fact. In the West, the miraculous events described in revered religious works are difficult for the average person to accept; even the most faithful can find themselves challenged no matter how much they want to believe. I'm not implying by any stretch that this memoir is in the category of those great religious accounts, but there are modern day miracles in this story, and some of them occurred in the United States.

For lack of memory and sometimes for convenience; I paraphrased conversations and repositioned the time when they took place, but the conversations and the events I wrote about were real. I say that now because I believe at some point you questioned the validity of this account.

There's something else. I grew up in the United States, in the West, where it's a fact that anything considered to be legitimate must be validated by scientific data. So it hasn't been easy for me to accept the things I now believe are totally true. I didn't realize how difficult my process of coming to the point of absolute belief was until years and many experiences later; experiences that I have shared with some close friends and a few family members, and perhaps a stranger here and there on the spur of the moment. I don't recall the exact moment when I finally accepted how deeply hesitant I was to tell the chapter of my life that you just read. Why was I hesitant? I had two solid and what I felt were very good reasons. One, I didn't want to be called crazy. Two, and perhaps what some might consider even worse, I didn't want to be seen as gullible. But obviously those fears no longer have a hold on me, and when I looked in the mirror before I began to write this book, and saw what I saw, I knew it was time.

For the past six years I had dealt with a darkening of the skin around my throat. So dark that it had been absolutely black at times. Most would simply sum it up as a medical condition, but I knew it was much more than that. You see, I am a proponent of Louise Hay's train of thought, meaning that emotional and mental factors can cause dis-ease. Yes, I acknowledge there was some kind of physical imbalance, but I believed the darkness was also the result of a deeper cause. There was a message for me in the dark skin that encased my neck for you see, I did not have the unmitigated courage to speak my truth as

I had witnessed it, to speak the truth of my experiences, and to speak my truth no matter who may or may not believe me. I believe my throat was literally packed with the decaying words I had been afraid to say, and those words had turned to poison.

For fifteen years I had hidden behind writing fiction, but the portion of my life that I wrote about in this memoir was as amazing as my fiction, and as the common saying goes, even stranger.

That brings me to my conclusion which focuses on a general mindset in my home country, America.

We enjoy many freedoms here; freedoms that I have an even greater appreciation for after traveling to numerous countries. In general we encourage exploration and individualism, and I acknowledge there's a certain kind of strength and stability in what the media calls Middle America. There is even a profound kindness for those in need in general, but especially if they remind us of ourselves. But I feel there is also something within us that needs to mature, for a tendency lies within the core psyche of many Americans to deem anything different, anything foreign as intrinsically wrong. There's a part of us that buys into the notion that if it wasn't established in this land, or at least in the West, it isn't acceptable. This is particularly true when it comes to religion and spirituality. God worshipped with pure hearts and peaceful actions in other countries around the world, under names that are unfamiliar to us can be labeled as not God at all, and in some cases as evil. I hope this memoir will help change that negative perception, if only to a minute degree.

And now I can tell you the darkness about my throat has all but disappeared.

www.ingramcontent.com/pod-product-compliance
Lightning Source LLC
Chambersburg PA
CBHW031247090426
42742CB00007B/350